STRATEGIES FOR EDUCATING AFRICAN AMERICAN CHILDREN

JUDITH ST.CLAIR HULL, PH.D.

Urban Ministries, Inc.

CHICAGO, ILLINOIS

Strategies for Educating African American Children

Publisher

UMI
(Urban Ministries, Inc.)
P.O. Box 436987
Chicago, IL 60643-6987
1-800-860-8642
www.urbanministries.com

First Edition
First Printing

Library of Congress Cataloging-in-Publication Data

Strategies for Educating African American Children/Judith St.Clair Hull, Ph.D.
Includes bibliographic references
ISBN 1-932715-79-7
ISBN 978-1-932715-79-8

1. Education. 2. Multicultural education 3. Christian education

Library of Congress Control Number: 2006932112

Printed in the United States of America.

STRATEGIES
FOR EDUCATING
AFRICAN AMERICAN
CHILDREN

CONTENTS

INTRODUCTION

Chuck enjoyed kids, so he said yes when he was asked to teach a Sunday School class of third graders. He remembered going to Sunday School when he was a boy and sitting in his grandmother's class. Since hers was the only teaching he was familiar with, Chuck taught just as his grandmother had.

There are many valuable things we can learn from those in the African American church who taught Sunday School in years past. Most African American Sunday School teachers used a lot of questions that prompted students to interact with the materials being taught. Teachers also viewed their students as part of the extended church family and took great interest in their development. The strengths of these teaching methods continue to be of great value today.

This book is designed to help you discover how to make the most of these traditional methods while offering some new ideas to assist you as a teacher. A skillful integration of the new with the old will help you become even more effective as a Sunday School teacher, a Vacation Bible School teacher, or a teacher of any other program in the African American church.

This book focuses on teaching children from 6 through 11 years of age. Boys and girls in this age bracket are called children—not little children or preteens, not junior highers or teenagers. These children are traditionally in grades one through six. In most Sunday Schools and church-education programs, these children are divided into two groups: primaries and juniors. Primaries are usually in grades one through three and range in age from 6 through 8. Juniors are 9 through 11 years of age and are usually in grades four through six.

Part I of this book is designed to increase our understanding of the children we are teaching. Chapter 1 gives us some general ideas about the way children learn. Understanding how children learn is the first step to knowing how to teach them. We may think we can teach children the same way we teach adults, only simplifying the material. However, this method will not work, because a child's understanding is not only simpler than an adult's; it is categorically different. For example, primaries understand concepts literally. When we say that God's Word is the seed, primaries typically visualize a very small seed of some kind that you plant in the ground.

In chapter 1, we will also examine different learning styles—what educators call *multiple intelligences*. One child may learn best through music; another, through art. Becoming familiar with these different learning styles can help us tailor our teaching methods to our students.

Finally, we will explore different levels of knowledge. Although we know that children do not think on the highest cognitive level, we want to begin teaching them critical thinking. Such thinking will help students navigate through the problems they will inevitably face in life.

Chapters 2 and 3 of part I present a developmental design of spiritual growth. God created us to learn in sequential steps or stages. Chapter 2 covers the stages of personality development for primaries and juniors. Visualize the personality as a hand with five fingers. The fingers represent the physical, mental, emotional, social, and moral aspects of the personality. The spirit is at the heart or center of a child's personality.

Chapter 3 deals with the holistic growth of a child's spirit. The three areas or components of spiritual development are cognitive (knowledge), affective (emotions and attitude), and volitional (behavior and actions). Well-rounded spiritual growth must take place in all three areas. In this chapter we will also discuss how primaries and juniors grow spiritually in each of these areas.

Part II is devoted to the art of Christian teaching. We will discuss not only the history of teaching children in the African American church but also the teaching styles that work best in this context. Chapter 4 gives an overview of the history of Sunday School in the African American church, which dates back to the very beginning of the Sunday School movement in the United States. In addition to the spiritual lessons children—and adults—learn in African American Sunday Schools, they also learn how to read and how to behave, as well as many other everyday skills needed for successful living.

In chapter 5, I present the findings of my research on the teaching methods African American Sunday School teachers use. During the fall of 1998, I conducted case studies consisting of three strong African American Sunday Schools in three diverse Black churches, from the inner city to suburbia, from Black Baptist to mainline Protestant. I observed the teachers in their particular environments and contexts and then conducted interviews with them and their superintendents. The names of the teachers who participated in my study have been changed to protect their identities. In chapter 6, I offer recommendations for building upon the strengths of Black teaching styles.

Part III gives practical guidelines for applying the material presented in parts I and II. Chapter 7 explains how to use teaching objectives. Objectives are necessary if we are to reach the specific educational goals we set for our students. If we have no goals, we will not know whether we have really accomplished anything in our teaching.

Chapter 8 is my favorite chapter of the book because leading children to Christ is the most important thing we can do. This chapter contains many of the principles I have learned and practiced throughout 40 years of teaching African American children and leading them to salvation in Christ.

Chapter 9 will give you a glimpse of one method of teaching: *cooperative learning*. This method is highly favored among African American Sunday School teachers because it is most congruent with Christian theology. We in the church should not be in competition with one another, but rather we are to help one another. As we teach, we want our methods to encourage students to work together.

Chapter 10 discusses how we can incorporate good reading methods into our teaching so that children can become strong readers of God's Word. Growing Christians need to be able to read, comprehend, and apply the teachings of the Bible. This is why African Americans have always made literacy instruction part of the Sunday School lesson, regardless of whether that goal is articulated.

Chapter 11, the grand finale, presents the components of a lesson plan in a straightforward, easy-to-understand way. Read this chapter and you will be ready to teach!

PART I:

UNDERSTANDING AFRICAN AMERICAN CHILDREN

CHAPTER 1

HOW CHILDREN LEARN

Sister Washington was thinking back over the 40 years she taught Sunday School. She was just 20 years old when she began teaching in the little storefront church her family attended. When she married, she and her husband began attending a much bigger church. Eventually she started teaching the primary class: boys and girls in grades one through three. She had expected the children in her new church to learn in different ways than the children in her previous church, but she soon discovered that the ways in which children learn are the same, no matter where they are.

Sister Washington attended a Sunday School teachers' convention each year and went to various workshops on teaching children, but mostly she developed her skills by teaching and interacting with the children at her church. In September of her first year as a teacher, very few of Sister Washington's first graders could read. She wanted the children to read their lessons aloud, but they were not able to do so.

Sister Washington loved teaching and caring for her primary students. It almost seemed that she became a substitute mother for her students during that hour in class. Sometimes a child would even forget and call her "Mama." During the winter season she helped the children with their boots, and there was always one child in the class who had not yet learned to tie his or her shoes.

Halfway through the Sunday School year, Sister Washington noticed that her third graders were changing in a big way. Pleasing their teacher was no longer the most important thing. Suddenly their peer group was more important. This new independence was exciting for her as a teacher too. Sister Washington was excited to see her students becoming more independent, and as a teacher, she shared their desire to experience new challenges. So when she was asked to teach the juniors—children in grades four, five, and six—she eagerly consented.

Maybe you had the good fortune of learning from a master teacher like Sister Washington. Maybe you already have much teaching experience yourself. Or maybe you are a brand-new teacher. Regardless of your level of teaching experience, it is important to keep in mind that good teachers are always learning, always seeking new and more effective ways to teach. This book is designed to help you do just that. In the chapters that follow, I will share not only what I have learned about teaching children from my own 40 years of experience in the field, but I will also offer observations of what other good teachers are doing as well as some principles that education specialists give us.

In this chapter we will examine what education specialists have to say about how children think and learn, and then we will explore the ways these principles can be applied to the Sunday School classroom.

The theories of education specialists can teach us a lot, but we need to keep in mind a few standards for evaluating those theories. First, we need to determine whether a given theory agrees with what the Bible teaches about human beings—both children and adults. God's Word helps us keep a realistic focus.

In the very beginning we see Adam and Eve in God's freshly created world (see Genesis 1–2). They were innocent and full of wonderful potential. We often see this same potential in our students.

But then Adam and Eve sinned and brought upon all humanity the tendency to do what is wrong. We can certainly see this in our students as well. When we excuse LeShaun to go to the bathroom and he mischievously takes a long detour, we see this sinful human nature in action.

Later in the New Testament, we read that the Lord Jesus came to redeem us. When we are saved, God clothes us in the righteousness of Christ and makes us new creations in Him (see Galatians 3:27 and 2 Corinthians 5:17). We look at ourselves and our tendency to sin, and we often wonder how God could see us as saints. But the truth is, He sees us with a new potential that comes when we accept Jesus as Savior. So when we look at our students, we see two sides: They are full of wonderful potential, and yet they have an inborn tendency to commit sin.

The second thing we need to do when we evaluate an educational theory is to make sure it stacks up against our own observations of how children learn. Does a particular theory seem to describe what you see happening in your classroom?

Finally, we need to be careful not to view any specific learning theory as "inspired." Sometimes educational theories sound so exciting that we try to rework our curriculum so that every aspect of what we teach conforms to the new theory. Educational theories can certainly help us become better teachers, but it is dangerous to put all our hopes in human-devised strategies. We need to evaluate learning theories through the lens of the Bible, to measure them against what we see in our students and in our own teaching styles, and then adapt the good parts and throw out the bad. In other words, "Eat the fish, but spit out the bones."

CHILDREN LEARN TO THINK ONE STEP AT A TIME

People often think that teaching children is just like teaching adults, only simpler. Nothing could be further from the truth. A child's thinking is different from an adult's. At each age level, children are developing new ways of understanding what is happening in their world. This is why Sunday School is organized in age-level classes.

As primaries and juniors develop, they are learning to understand the world around them from a cognitive, or an intellectual, thinking perspective. Jean Piaget, a Swiss educator and child psychologist, had much to say about the intellectual development of children. His emphasis on cognitive learning—the area that deals with facts—is useful in helping us understand how children learn. Cognitive learning is one of the most important components of a Sunday School or church-education program. Boys and girls need to learn what the Bible says, understand its meaning, and apply it to their lives.

According to Piaget, children from the ages of 7 through 12 are in the stage of *concrete intellectual operations* (Piaget 1967, 39–57). During this developmental stage, children are capable of using reason in acts of the will. This means that they can think through whether an action or behavior is the right or wrong thing to do. Prior to this age, children make behavioral choices based primarily upon what gives them pleasure. However, since primaries and juniors can choose what is right, they can understand that God has laws that must be obeyed and that disobeying them is sin. Christian educators call this the *age of accountability*. In other words, at this point in their lives, children become accountable to God for the wrong things they do. They are also accountable for what they do with the message of salvation.

During the primary and junior years, children understand what rules are and recognize that they can participate in creating them. Sunday School teachers will find that if they sit down with their students at the beginning of the school year and develop class rules, the children will gain an understanding of how rules are created and will work together to make sure the rules are obeyed.

Primaries and juniors are also able to generalize their understanding by taking what they have learned in one situation and applying it to similar situations. For instance, primaries can take a story they have heard about a child who is kind to someone with a physical challenge and then apply this principle of kindness to others who have a variety of physical or mental limitations. Juniors are even better at applying the truths of Scripture to a variety of situations. Teachers can help primaries and juniors develop this skill by telling open-ended stories or using case studies in which students are asked to think through the life applications of the Scripture lessons.

During the primary and junior years, children develop a sense of fairness as they first experience personal injustice, whether actual or imagined. Although they will not be able to understand the more abstract concept of justice, they will understand fairness. Teachers of this age group may hear their students complain, "You always pick the boys [or girls] first!" Although this perception may be more imagined than real, it demonstrates that primaries and juniors are developing more discernment about the fairness of a situation.

Piaget believed that somewhere around the age of seven, children begin to consider the viewpoints of others and reflect on the objections others express. Of course, there are hints of this kind of thinking even during the preschool years, but primaries and juniors can truly be said to have reached this stage. Primaries and juniors who have developed this skill are able to work on projects requiring cooperation, and they are learning to collaborate with others. Sunday School teachers can plan projects on which primary-age children will need to work together, such as building the walls around the city of Jericho using toy blocks. Juniors can do simple research projects, such as interviewing church members and then working together to prepare a report on the history of the local church.

Piaget primarily studied cognitive learning, but learning is much more than head knowledge. To limit learning to cognition alone would be to diminish the wonderful riches of human learning and development. Cognitive learning is an important part of spiritual growth, but we should not confine ourselves to such a narrow perspective of learning. Let's look at some of the other types of learning.

CHILDREN LEARN IN A VARIETY OF WAYS

God has blessed us with many different types of intelligence or "learning styles." We all know mathematical geniuses, brilliant musicians, gifted artists, and others who are highly skilled and talented. We learn in different ways, and we each have different strengths.

In his book, *Frames of Mind: The Theory of Multiple Intelligences,* Howard Gardner, an education professor at Harvard University, described seven different types of intelligence (Gardner 1983, 59–239). The first type is called *linguistic intelligence* or the ability to use words. This is the kind of intelligence we associate with success in school. People who are gifted in this area know how to use words well. They may be proficient in writing, understanding written material, giving oral presentations, and debating. They are sensitive to the sounds, rhythms, and functions of language. Although there are many forms of language use, Gardner thought that the highest form was poetry.

Verbal learning is of special importance in Christian education, although it is not the only area of spiritual learning. God uses the medium of His written Word to communicate with us, so we need to learn what the Bible says through reading and listening. Although teachers predominantly use words in the classroom, we often neglect some of the higher verbal expressions, such as poetry. Encourage juniors to respond to a lesson with poems that they can read aloud to their classmates.

Educators have also discovered that keeping a journal is a wonderful way to develop linguistic abilities. We want our students to be able to easily express themselves in writing. Journalizing is also a great way to teach juniors to communicate with God.

Some teachers tell their students to write down their prayer requests and keep a record of the answers. Others tell their students to write down all their thoughts about God and His work in their lives. This type of journal is like a spiritual diary.

The second type of intelligence is *logical/mathematical/scientific intelligence,* which combines mathematical and scientific abilities. One of the responsibilities that we as Christian teachers have is to nurture the talents and gifts of our students. Consequently, we must look for ways to use a variety of intelligences in our teaching. Primaries and juniors will find simple arithmetic problems in Bible lessons, such as the story of the shepherd who had 100 sheep and lost one of them. Asking how many sheep were left in the sheepfold gives children with mathematical intelligence a chance to shine and to feel affirmed in the gift God has given them. Children with this gift may also be chosen to count the class offering.

Science is an even more useful tool in the classroom. Discovering the wonders of God's creation can help us worship Him in a deeper way. Teachers and students can bring wonderful samples of God's creation to class: a caterpillar in a cocoon, a beautiful bouquet of flowers, a discarded bird's nest, and so forth. To see things, feel them, and even smell them evokes a feeling of awe that causes us to worship the Lord. Sometimes these experiences are more effective in leading children to worship God than mere words can ever be.

Science is the description of God's creation. This was the task God gave Adam (Genesis 2:19). Even primary students will enjoy and profit from simple scientific experiments, such as placing a piece of paper in a foil pan, setting the paper on fire, and seeing what happens. This will help children understand the miracle of the burning bush that burned and burned but did not burn up.

The third type of intelligence Gardner described is *musical intelligence.* This gift includes listening, performing, and composing. Musical talents seem to emerge earlier in life than any other ability. Some children may be embarrassed by a lack of reading skills, but they can participate in and demonstrate excellence in the area of music. Read the book of Psalms to see how believers are encouraged to express love for God in a variety of musical forms. Primaries and juniors can joyfully express love to God through music. Most children in this age group also enjoy performing for the church body. They can even compose simple tunes to help them with their memory verses.

The fourth type of intelligence is *spatial/art/architecture/engineering intelligence.* Children who are gifted in this area can assemble a puzzle, draw a picture, or use engineering and architectural skills to create a play road for toy cars. Children, like adults, enjoy doing things they excel at, but by engaging the entire class in these activities, the lesson will be more interesting for all the students. This kind of intelligence can be incorporated into teaching in a variety of ways. Students can create jigsaw puzzles from Bible visuals, mix up the pieces, and then reassemble them. Art in a variety of forms, such as painting pictures of events that happened in a Bible story or making gifts for others to show generosity and kindness, can reinforce the truths of the lesson. The more art media we use, the more enjoyable and profitable the art activities will be for spatially gifted children. When supervised with care, such activities as cutting, pasting, and using markers, crayons, and even watercolors can be incorporated into Sunday School lessons.

During Vacation Bible School and in other Christian-education settings, children can participate in projects that are even more creative. One summer our church had a backyard Bible club. We set out an old dishpan with about a half inch of finger paint inside and gave each child a large piece of blank newsprint (mural paper). Then each child stepped barefoot into the finger paint and walked across the paper to illustrate "I will follow Jesus." A dishpan filled with warm soapy water was at the other end of the yard, along with old bath towels and a teenage volunteer to assist with cleanup. Neither the children nor the teachers soon forgot this illustration.

The fifth type of intelligence is *bodily movement intelligence.* This involves moving the body in dance or as a tool, and even moving to use tools. Dance is the highest form of this intelligence. Recently, churches have rediscovered dance as a means of worship, and many churches have creative dance groups for children. Learning to worship in this manner is a wonderful expression of this gift. However, the church helper who repairs plumbing, builds shelves for the church library, and adjusts the equipment that records the Sunday morning service is also using this talent for the Lord.

Children enjoy watching acts of service and even helping a bit, although they may miss out on some activities that can be done only on weekdays. But once again, what is most important is that we as teachers encourage all our students to develop their skills for God's glory.

The last two types of intelligence that Gardner describes are *interpersonal intelligence and intrapersonal intelligence.* Interpersonal intelligence has to do with the emotions children feel individually and their ability to put those feelings into words. Children with this ability are also able to understand the feelings of others. We can help children develop in this area by discussing how they think various Bible characters felt or by discussing the feelings of children in application stories. All Christians need to develop greater empathy for the feelings of others. Primaries and juniors are just entering the stage when they are capable of growth in this area.

Intrapersonal intelligence is the ability to work with groups of people to bring about great good in our world. Martin Luther King Jr. is an excellent example of someone who had this particular gift. Public school teachers and administrators are also gifted in this area, as are many people in leadership positions. Older primaries and juniors are often interested in learning to be leaders. Teachers can help children develop leadership and collaboration skills by giving assignments to groups of children, observing how they interact, and sharing ideas to help the groups function better. Teachers can also designate different children as group leaders in order to develop each child's potential in this area. Intrapersonal intelligence is one of the more useful intelligences in the functioning of the church body, and children will profit greatly from opportunities to develop group skills.

Gardner has shown us that there are many more types of intelligence than those measured by school IQ tests. Having a broad view of learning is necessary for a more comprehensive spiritual education of our students. We can respect and encourage many different kinds of gifts and talents. Since God views us this way, we should view our students this way as well. We also want to affirm and encourage our students by utilizing a wide variety of teaching methods, no matter what types of intelligence or gifts they have. However, it is dangerous to assume that all of these paths of learning are equal when it comes to the Christian education of children. We need to choose those modes of intelligence that are appropriate for the objectives we seek to achieve. If we want to teach biblical facts, then we will emphasize the linguistic mode (whether spoken or written), although we may use other modes, such as music, for reinforcement. If our objective is worship, we may primarily use music, dance, and words that express beauty and emotion. To stimulate the wonder and awe of our Creator, we can employ the art of science. Some areas of intelligence, such as mathematics, will not be used very often in Sunday School classes because such gifts are not as useful in teaching Bible lessons.

CHILDREN CAN LEARN TO THINK ON HIGHER LEVELS

Beginning teachers often focus primarily on rote learning; that is, just teaching children to remember the verbal and written lesson material and to recite the Bible memory verse. But thinking is much more complex than simple rote memory. How can we teach our students to think on higher levels? First, we have to analyze the different types and levels of thinking. Fortunately for us, Benjamin S. Bloom did that more than 40 years ago. Bloom and a team of other educational psychologists devised an outline of levels of cognitive thinking (Bloom 1994, 1–18). Visualize yourself standing at the bottom of a staircase. Each step or level of cognition you ascend builds upon the steps beneath it.

Bloom classified *knowledge*—the basic acquisition of information—as the lowest level of thinking. The emphasis of acquiring such information is on rote memory. Although knowledge is the lowest level of cognition, it is the foundation on which all other levels of thinking rest. At this level, children learn to quote a Bible verse, but they may not be able to understand it. Teachers will often ask questions about the details of the Bible lesson to help their students retain the information. Although this level of knowledge is very basic, it is necessary for children to learn the facts of Scripture and remember what happened in the lesson. Verbal repetition will often help students remember basic facts.

Now climb one step on the staircase. The second level of thinking is *understanding*, which has to do with understanding the meaning of cognitive material. Since children are often able to repeat facts and other information without understanding what they are saying, we definitely want primaries and juniors to progress beyond this basic level of thinking. Teachers need to learn to explain new information in ways children can understand, and they need to be continually checking to see that the children truly understand what they are being taught. Teachers may think they can tell when children really understand a concept, but they might be surprised if they probed a little deeper. A good teacher will ask these kinds of questions: "What is _____?" "What does _____ mean?" "Can you say that in your own words?" Well-formulated questions can often tell us whether our students really understand the lesson.

Climb up another level to the third step. This level of thinking is *application*. We define this as applying knowledge to new situations. This level calls upon students to remember what they have learned, to understand it, and to apply it. Application is an important component of Bible lessons. Jesus said that we are His friends if we do what He commands (John 15:14). If we want our primaries and juniors to do what God wants them to do, they must develop the thinking skills to apply God's Word to their own life situations. We can help them do this by relating stories of contemporary children just like them and asking them what the children in these stories should do. Then you might ask, "Now what would you do in this situation?" In order to obey God's Word, children must first learn how to apply it to their own lives.

Now move up to the fourth step. This level of thinking is *analysis*. It is described as breaking down the material into its constituent parts, seeing the relationship between those parts, and detecting the ways they are organized. When juniors learn how to outline material, they are thinking in the analytical realm. In the spiritual realm, juniors can learn to outline the weekly portion of Scripture they have been assigned. Even primaries learn to analyze Bible stories when they arrange the parts of a story in correct sequential order.

Now climb the next step. *Synthesis*, the fifth level of thinking, is defined as putting together the elements and parts of something to form a whole. This is a creative level of thinking in which the parts are assembled to constitute a pattern or structure not clearly seen before. If analysis is looking at the individual trees of the forest and categorizing them, synthesis is taking the analysis of the individual trees and seeing in it a pattern that describes the whole forest. Although this is a very advanced level of thinking, even primaries can learn to think on this level. Give the children short stories to read or tell Bible stories and ask them to think of a title that will describe what the story is about. Thinking on this level will help students see the overall truths of the Bible without getting hung up on distortions that emphasize a verse here or a verse there.

Finally, we have reached the top step. *Evaluation*, the sixth level of thinking, is defined as the ability to make judgments about the value of ideas, work, solutions, methods, materials, and so forth. Criteria must be developed upon which to make the judgment. The goal of Christian education is to produce believers who are able to look at all of Scripture and base their lives upon it.

Although we cannot expect primaries and juniors to think in-depth on all those levels, we do want to challenge them as far as their thinking will go. Sometimes we call evaluation "critical thinking." This kind of thinking goes all the way to the top of the staircase. Critical thinking is needed for African American people to experience true empowerment. True liberation cannot be brought about simply by teaching truths from an African American perspective. African Americans need to see beyond what they are told about themselves and their world.

The civil-rights battles of the sixties and seventies were born in the Black church. Today racism has taken even more insidious forms, so new weapons and strategies are needed. We are training up new generations that will meet new struggles, so we need to develop students who are able to think critically about their world and apply biblical solutions to the troubles of their generation.

Reference List

Bloom, Benjamin S. et al. Excerpts from the "Taxonomy of educational objectives, the classification of educational goals, Handbook I: Cognitive domain." *Bloom's Taxonomy: A Forty-Year Retrospective. Vol. 2, Ninety-third Yearbook of the National Society for the Study of Education.* Edited by Lorin W. Anderson and Lauren A. Sosniak. Chicago: The University of Chicago Press, 1994.

Gardner, Howard. *Frames of Mind: The Theory of Multiple Intelligences.* New York: Basic Books, Inc. Publishers, 1983.

Piaget, Jean. *Six Psychological Studies.* Translated by Anita Tezer. New York: Random House, 1967.

CHAPTER 2

PERSONALITY DEVELOPMENT

Have you ever tried to guess the ages of children by looking at their teeth? Preschoolers have tiny baby teeth. At about 5 or 6 years of age, the two front teeth come out for those famous "gap-toothed" smiles. Then the big permanent teeth come in, teeth that look much too big for 6- and 7-year-olds. But just as children's teeth come out and grow in at different ages and rates, their personalities also develop differently. We must be careful not to stereotype the stages of personality development by assuming that children's personalities will develop in exactly the same way. Doing so may limit their growth potential. However, knowing the stages of personality development can help us greatly as teachers by giving us some ideas about how our students are learning and progressing. With that in mind, in the pages that follow I will present an outline of how children's personalities develop.

Ted Ward, a Christian educator, likes to represent the five aspects of the personality as five fingers on a hand (Ward 1989, 18). The first finger represents the physical aspect of the personality; the second, the mental; the third, the emotional; the fourth, the social; and the fifth, the moral. You may be wondering whether there should be a sixth finger to represent the spiritual aspect. Ward's simple device shows us that all the fingers are part of the hand. Then what do we call the palm? The palm represents the spiritual aspect. (We will discuss spiritual development in more detail in the next chapter.) The center of every being is the spirit. As teachers we are not able to directly access a child's spirit. Only the Holy Spirit is able to do this. Instead, we must go through the various aspects of the personality in order to reach the spirits of our students.

Let's look at the five aspects of the personality as they relate to primaries and juniors, examining the characteristics and educational implications of each aspect. (See Figures 1 and 2 at the end of this chapter.)

PHYSICAL CHARACTERISTICS

As I mentioned in the introduction, primaries are children from ages 6 through 8 who are in the first, second, and third grades. Primaries do not grow as rapidly as they did in their preschool years. Although their large- and small-muscle coordination is increasing, their hand-eye coordination is not fully developed. They cannot color within small spaces, nor should we expect them to. Just like preschoolers, they prefer action to observation, but they tire easily.

Teachers need to consider the physical characteristics of primaries when planning the lesson and incorporate physical activities to help students learn verses and achieve other objectives. Lesson plans need to alternate quiet and active tasks. Special adaptations are needed for younger primaries, such as giving them large sheets of paper so they can draw big pictures or trace big letters.

Juniors—children in the fourth, fifth, and sixth grades—are beginning to grow more rapidly. They also experience periods of high energy alternating with periods of fatigue. They are generally healthy and have greater muscle coordination. Church ministry activities for juniors should exercise their high energy rather than repress it.

Some juniors, especially girls, may enter puberty as young as 9 years of age. Teachers should point to biblical role models when teaching juniors what it means to be male or female. Teachers should also encourage their students to emulate Christian men and women as contemporary role models, recognizing that they themselves are role models for their students.

MENTAL CHARACTERISTICS

Thanks to Swiss psychologist Jean Piaget, we know a great deal about the mental development of children. Primaries think very literally and concretely. For instance, when we talk about a "fisher of men," a primary might picture someone using a fishing pole to catch people. Primaries also have good imaginations, so we can ask them to visualize things as long as our descriptions are very literal. For instance, we can encourage them to use their imaginations to understand what is happening in a Bible story. They will also enjoy acting out Bible stories and the character traits we are teaching. Primaries learn of God's character as they learn of His actions. Young primaries love school and learning. They will even spend large portions of their leisure time playing school. In the first grade they are just learning to read and write, but by the end of the third grade, they will be pretty good readers and writers. Since most primaries like to read and write, we should encourage them to build upon these skills. We also need to keep in mind that primaries do not understand the grand sweep of historical sequence, so we do not need to worry about telling Bible stories in historical order. However, they are capable of arranging the events of a single story in correct sequence.

We cannot expect first graders to be able to read large amounts of material. At the very beginning of first grade, children are just learning to read a few words, so they may not know how to read anything beyond their own names. Even second and third graders, who have a rapidly increasing reading vocabulary, read slowly and haltingly. (Some children like to read as fast as they can recognize the words, but this is not necessarily better, as they tend to trip over words in their haste and do not convey the meaning through their intonation and phrasing.) Reading is important for primaries, but it is always best if the teacher reads the story first in an exciting and smooth manner. When the teacher tells the story first, the children will not only understand it better, but they will also find it more interesting. Then when the children read the story for themselves, they will be reviewing the material and will be more likely to remember it.

Teachers need to remember that very few children read at the exact level expected for their grade. Some children read above their grade level, while others read below it. Sunday School and other church classes give children a good opportunity to expand upon their reading abilities. Children should find reading at church to be a great help and encouragement in improving their reading skills. More will be said about incorporating reading into the classroom in chapter 10, "Reading the Word."

During the primary years we begin to introduce map reading skills. First, we may ask each child to draw a picture of their home. Then on a table-sized piece of paper, we draw the church and the surrounding streets and have each of the children place their house on their street. The children can then use two fingers to "walk" from their houses to the church. This is especially effective if all of the children live near the church. If the children live farther away, they can pretend they are driving to church from their homes.

Teachers may also introduce simple Bible maps in their lessons. Primaries do not yet understand the great distances between places, but they can look for names of places as a reading activity.

Primaries are also learning to classify information. Most importantly, they can distinguish between true stories and make-believe. This is the age when children discover the truth about Santa Claus, the Easter Bunny, the Tooth Fairy, and superheroes. Primary teachers need to help primaries understand that Bible stories are true.

Primaries can also classify other categories, such as size, color, age, and gender. Another characteristic of the mental development of primaries is their growing attention spans. If a Bible story is told in an absorbing manner, primaries should be able to listen for 10 to 15 minutes. Active involvement increases the length of the attention span.

Compared with primary-age children, the thinking skills of juniors are rapidly increasing. At this stage they are fully engaged in concrete reasoning. They can learn structure and organization and can reason beyond simple factual knowledge. They can pay attention for longer periods, and they should have good reading skills by now. If not, they will tend to have low self-esteem, especially in a school context. At this stage children are beginning to demonstrate special talents and aptitudes. Most juniors can read Sunday School lessons and short passages from the Bible by this time. They should also be able to write short paragraphs.

Teachers need to take into account the growing mental abilities of juniors and help them develop their reasoning power. One of the ways this can be done is by asking questions that make use of critical thinking skills, such as asking children to analyze and apply the teachings of the Bible.

Most juniors are able to learn the books of the Bible, the divisions of the Old and New Testaments, and how to find specific Scripture passages. Although their map-reading skills are not highly developed, the use of maps can help them remember information. Juniors are also learning how to think beyond the basic facts of the Bible and apply what they read to their own lives.

EMOTIONAL CHARACTERISTICS

Primaries do not like criticism, but they will respond well to praise when they do something right or well. They are often afraid of many things. Some are afraid of the dark, some of bugs, some of thunderstorms, and some of dogs. Teachers need to talk gently to primaries about their fears, without ridiculing or belittling them. We need to remind primaries that Jesus is always with us, taking care of us. Because primaries are emotional and dramatic, they enjoy dramatizing Bible stories and Christian behavior. But teachers need to assign parts to students that will emphasize good conduct and character, because the behaviors they act out will be firmly engraved in their memories. (For instance, we can assign children the part of the Good Samaritan, but if we assign them the parts of the thieves and robbers, we will be teaching our students that mistreating others is fun.) Primaries are also learning to sympathize with others, an important trait for Christians. We can encourage this by asking the children how certain individuals will feel when they are hurt.

Juniors can be very emotional and may have frequent outbursts. Some may feel inadequate or inferior, so it is important for them to feel a sense of accomplishment. Teachers can help by assigning projects that are sufficiently difficult so that juniors can be proud of their accomplishments, but not so difficult that students will fail.

Creative art activities help juniors express their emotions. While we may steer away from messier projects on Sunday mornings, we can include these kinds of activities in Vacation Bible School and weekday clubs when the children are dressed more casually and have more time to paint, model clay, and so forth. Even during Sunday School, children can enjoy some creative coloring, pasting, and cutting. We should not view these activities as just time fillers. Emotions and art are gifts from God. He created all that is beautiful in our world. When children create beautiful things, they can be pointed to the God who made all these things and can be prompted to worship Him. And when they draw pictures to illustrate feelings (such as how Nicodemus felt when he talked with Jesus in John 3:1–21, or how children in the Bible may have felt when they were sick), their perspectives of Scripture is enhanced.

Juniors also enjoy children's choir as a means of expression. Teachers can encourage individual musical gifts and other talents by giving children special assignments that make use of their abilities. One child can sing a solo for the church; another can draw a picture for a Sunday School program cover. In this way we can appreciate the emotional expressiveness of juniors rather than squelching their wonderful personalities.

SOCIAL CHARACTERISTICS

Primaries are very sociable and like to talk with others. Involving primaries in discussion will help them develop this skill. Around 8 years of age, they begin to enjoy belonging to a group. For this reason, and because they do not like losing, it is best not to focus on individual competition during this stage. Instead, teach the children using team methods so they can begin to function as a group in Sunday School. (See chapter 9 for detailed information on structuring lessons for teams or groups.) Individual competition may pressure children to try to succeed, but they may feel so depressed when they lose that they may not try the next time.

Learning to function as a group in Sunday School is also more in tune with biblical theology. God desires that we work together, not against one another, so we need to plan activities that will encourage primaries to work together. For instance, we can divide the children into learning pairs so they can help each other with the weekly memory verse. Or separate the class into two groups to assemble puzzles you have created out of the weekly Bible visual aid. Even art can be done as a group, such as creating a mural or working together on some other large project. When we design group activities, students can be learning to work together while they are reviewing a Bible story, a verse, or some other biblical content.

Because primaries like to help, include jobs your students can handle so they will learn responsibility. Be aware that primaries sometimes forget to follow through, so you may need to remind them to finish any assigned tasks.

Juniors like the socialization of groups or clubs. At this stage in their development, they are capable of group sharing and cooperation and can recognize the viewpoints of others. Even though they are beginning to understand one another, they also tend to have more physical and verbal conflicts. They are also especially vulnerable to the lure of the wrong crowd. But this is a great opportunity for teachers to minister to juniors. Juniors appreciate teachers and club leaders who are there for them more than just one hour a week. A skilled and caring teacher will work to build a team with the students in his or her class. If the fellowship of Christian children is strong enough, juniors will be able to withstand pressures to join groups that get into trouble. Teachers can redirect the desire of their students to be part of a group that might lead them in the wrong direction by starting them on the road to becoming part of the church family—the family of God. Instead of joining the wrong crowd, students can be encouraged to find a social group, a community, in their Sunday School class, at Vacation Bible School, or in a weekday Bible club.

The social characteristics of juniors point to the value of teaching them collaborative learning skills. Juniors can be dependable and responsible. Although some of the suggestions for primaries will work for juniors, juniors can learn to function in more complex group roles and to develop group leadership skills. One way to give juniors the opportunity to develop in these areas is to divide the class into several groups and assign different roles to each child, such as recorder, listener, and leader. (See chapter 9 for details on how this works.)

Because the peer group is so important to juniors, they are very sensitive to how others view them. Teachers will want to avoid situations that make some students appear as "losers."

MORAL CHARACTERISTICS

Primaries believe strongly in rules and will hardly ever allow them to be changed. Therefore, primaries can understand that God has rules and that He rewards those who obey them and punishes those who disobey. They will sometimes ask about death, heaven, who made the devil, what color God is, and other tricky questions. Primary teachers need to think through these issues carefully and ask God for help in answering their students' questions.

At the beginning of the quarter or school year, spend time with your primaries and juniors helping them develop class rules. As the children suggest a rule, ask them why it would make a good rule. Discuss the punishment or consequences they think rule breakers should receive. When children are involved in establishing rules, they will learn about the process of rule making, they will better understand the purpose of rules, and they will be more willing to obey them. As problems occur in the classroom, more rules may need to be added during another rule-making session.

Because primaries understand the concept of rules and the consequences of breaking those rules, they can understand a simple explanation of the way of salvation—that because we have broken God's rules, we need to be saved (or born again). (See the chapter on "Leading Children to Christ" for help in applying age-specific characteristics when you explain salvation to children.)

Primaries have a very elementary understanding of race. While preschoolers identify skin colors and maybe a few other race-specific characteristics, primaries can see that there are many shades of Black as well as other physical differences among Black people. One primary insisted that her mother was White, not because of the shade of her skin, but because she had freckles.

Our main task as teachers is to help primaries develop a healthy image of being Black. If we emphasize the injustices that Black people experience, young children will tend to feel a great hurt deep within their souls. Primaries need to be shown positive images of Black Christians in the Bible and in contemporary life before they hear of the suffering and victimization of African Americans.

Juniors have a great concern for fairness—the rigid application of rules. Although their zeal for fairness is not based upon an understanding of social justice, it signifies that juniors are beginning to develop moral reasoning. This ability can be broadened and developed through stories in which juniors discuss a moral dilemma and choose the best solution. Teachers should ask students why their decisions are the best choice. Teachers should also foster a classroom environment in which students feel free to ask questions.

Juniors are just beginning to understand the concept of race. At this stage they can see that race is something that binds people together as a team. African American juniors can understand that in this country there are many different "teams" or races and ethnic groups. As juniors identify with African Americans as a group, they are ready to learn about the suffering as well as the glory.

Juniors can also identify with heroes, so we need to provide them with African biblical heroes, Black history heroes, and contemporary Christian heroes. African

American teachers also can be wonderful role models for primaries and juniors to follow. Since fairness is important to juniors, we can hold up African American role models who have contributed positively to righting injustice in our world. We do not want to teach our children to hate people who are not Black, but we want them to feel empowered to seek what is truly fair.

With this understanding of how our students' personalities develop, we can go on to the next chapter to learn how primaries and juniors develop spiritually.

Reference List

Ward, Ted. *Values Begin at Home.* Wheaton, Illinois: Victor Books, a Division of Scripture Press Publications, Inc., 1989.

EDUCATION FOR THE
WHOLE PERSONALITY: PRIMARY

	Characteristics	Implications
Physical	• Prefer action to observation. • Eye-hand coordination not fully developed. • Tire easily.	• Incorporate physical activities to help students learn verses and achieve other objectives. • Alternate quiet and active tasks. • Give younger primaries large sheets of paper so they can draw big pictures or trace big letters.
Mental	• Think very literally and concretely. • Have good imaginations. • Love school and learning. • Learning to read and write. • Enjoy acting out a Bible story. • Unable to place historical events in sequential order, but they can place the events in a story in correct sequence. • Do not understand large distances, but they can look for names of places on a map. • Learning to classify. • Learning the difference between true and make-believe. • Attention span increasing.	• Encourage children to use their imaginations to understand what is happening in a Bible story. • Incorporate dramatizations of Bible stories and Christian conduct. • Give children ample opportunities to read and write. • Avoid using figures of speech, such as "Ask Jesus into your heart." • Provide opportunities for students to arrange the sequence of events in a story. • Read a story to students before having them read it for themselves. • Teach God's character through stories of His acts. • Tailor activities for the different reading and writing levels of students. • Introduce very simple map-reading activities.
Emotional	• Do not accept criticism well. • Respond well to praise. • Have many fears. • Very emotional and dramatic. • Enjoy acting out Bible stories and Christian behavior. • Learning to sympathize with others.	• Use positive reinforcement. • Teach primaries about God's continuing presence and care for them. • Involve children in drama and assign roles that will emphasize good conduct and character.
Social	• Very sociable and like to talk with others. • Enjoy belonging to a group. • Do not like to lose. • Like to help. • Can take responsibility but may forget things.	• Focus on group activities that encourage cooperation. • Avoid activities that promote individual competition. • Give students jobs to foster responsibility, but be prepared to remind students to follow through. • Involve primaries in discussion.
Moral	• Believe strongly in rules and resist changing them. • Sometimes ask tricky questions about spiritual issues, such as heaven. • Understand the concept of consequences for breaking rules. • Have a very elementary understanding of race. Can see that there are many shades of Blackness. • Need to develop a healthy image of being Black	• Involve students in developing classroom rules. • Teach that God rewards good behavior and is pleased when students do what is right. • Teach about consequences of disobeying. • Answer students' questions about heaven and other spiritual matters. • Help students develop a healthy image of being Black. • Present positive images of Black Christians in the Bible and in contemporary life.

Figure 1. Primary Characteristics and Related Implications

EDUCATION FOR THE
WHOLE PERSONALITY: JUNIOR

	Characteristics	Implications
Physical	• Entering a period of rapid growth. • Experience periods of high energy alternating with periods of fatigue. • Generally in good health. • Have greater muscle coordination. • May enter puberty as young as 9 years of age.	• Plan activities that use the high energy of juniors rather than repress it. • Provide biblical and contemporary role models of what it means to be male or female.
Mental	• Thinking skills are rapidly increasing. • Can engage in concrete reasoning. • Can learn structure and organization. • Can learn to reason beyond simple facts. • Have a longer attention span. • Should have developed good reading skills. If not, they can have low self-esteem. • Can write short paragraphs. • Able to analyze and apply teachings from the Bible. • Able to learn books of the Bible and can find specific Bible passages. • Map-reading skills are not fully developed. • Special aptitudes becoming apparent.	• Integrate reading skills into the lessons and encourage supplementary reading. • Structure and organize Bible learning through discovery and organizers. • Use map lessons to help juniors remember information. • Teach the books of the Bible and the two divisions of the Bible as well as how to find Scripture passages. • Use questions to help juniors analyze and apply the teachings of the Bible to their own lives.
Emotional	• Tend to be emotional and may have frequent outbursts. • May feel inadequate or inferior. • Need to feel a sense of accomplishment. • Enjoy expressing their emotions through creative art and music.	• Assign activities that will promote a sense of accomplishment. • Encourage individual music gifts and other talents. • Use a variety of creative art activities to help students express their emotions and worship God.
Social	• Like the socialization of groups. • Capable of group sharing and cooperation. • Can recognize the viewpoints of others and are beginning to understand one another. • May be vulnerable to the lure of the wrong crowd. • May have physical and verbal conflicts. • Can be dependable and responsible. • Can learn to function in more complex group roles and to develop group leadership skills. • May be competitive but have trouble with self-confidence.	• Teach cooperative learning skills. • Create a community within the Bible class to counteract the pull of groups that might lead students in the wrong direction. • Teach conflict resolution skills. • Use activities that develop group leadership skills and teach students how to function in more complex group roles. • Teach at age-appropriate level to develop students' self-confidence.
Moral	• Have great concern for fairness. • Have not yet developed an understanding of social justice. • Have begun to develop moral reasoning. • Have begun to understand the concept of race. • Can identify with heroes.	• Develop moral reasoning through true-to-life stories that present moral dilemmas. • Teach about African biblical heroes, Black history heroes, and contemporary Christian heroes. • Foster a classroom environment in which juniors feel free to ask questions. • Provide examples of Black role models who have contributed positively to righting injustice.

Figure 2. Junior Characteristics and Related Implications

CHAPTER 3

SPIRITUAL DEVELOPMENT

"What is spiritual maturity?" According to the Bible, when we become believers, we need to "leave the elementary teachings about Christ and go on to maturity" (Hebrews 6:1). Before we consider how children develop spiritually, let's consider what constitutes spiritual maturity for Christians of any age. Some will say that having a great knowledge of the Bible is absolute proof of spiritual maturity; others will say that it is demonstrated by heartfelt singing and praying; and still others say that showing love is the ultimate evidence. But the Bible takes a balanced approach to spiritual development.

THREE AREAS OF SPIRITUAL GROWTH

Regardless of a person's age, spiritual development needs to be well-balanced and holistic. The goal of a church-education program is for every member of the body of Christ to achieve well-balanced spiritual maturity. Holistic spiritual development can be represented as an equilateral triangle. Each corner of the triangle represents one of the three realms or areas of spiritual development: the cognitive (intellectual knowledge), the affective (emotions and attitude), and the volitional (actions).

This illustration also emphasizes three truths about spiritual development. First, when an equilateral triangle is rotated, all the corners still look exactly alike. This means that no one corner or area of spiritual development is more important than the other two. Second, a triangle's sides connect at each corner, which shows us that the three areas of spiritual development are not compartmentalized but are connected to one another, forming one cohesive whole. Finally, just as an equilateral triangle is multidirectional, spiritual maturity must also progress in all three directions. Figure 3 at the end of this chapter demonstrates how the various areas of spiritual development fit into the triangle and are related to one another.

Growth in the Area of Spiritual Knowledge

First let's consider spiritual development of the intellect—cognitive spiritual growth. In Romans 12:2 we learn that the Bible is the source of spiritual knowledge and has the power to transform our thinking.

Spiritual knowledge encompasses everything from the basic facts of the Bible to theological reasoning. Biblical knowledge involves more than just rote memorization of words. The highest level of development in this area involves the ability to discern the meaning of biblical truth and apply God's Word to all areas of life. For instance, when we learn the doctrinal truths about the deity of Christ, His death on the cross, and His miraculous resurrection from the dead, we are able to discern the errors in the many false doctrines. At that level of spiritual development, mature Christians are able to arm themselves against the tricks of the devil (Ephesians 6:17). But if we only concern ourselves with an intellectual knowledge of God, we will be very unbalanced as Christians. Even devils believe in God and tremble (James 2:19). But their belief is only simple cognition and does not penetrate the heart or actions.

Growth in the Area of Spiritual Attitude

The second area of spiritual development is in the affective realm. This involves heart attitude, including a person's emotions, values, and thoughts. God desires our wholehearted love and gives us this promise: "You will seek me and find me when you seek me with all your heart" (Jeremiah 29:13). David prayed, "Create in me a pure heart, O God, and renew a steadfast spirit within me" (Psalm 51:10). He also asked,

> "Who may ascend the hill of the LORD?
> Who may stand in his holy place?
> He who has clean hands and a pure heart"
> (from Psalm 24:3–4).

We cannot approach God or enter into His presence without clean hearts. African Americans, as a people, have grown close to God through celebratory worship, which is the essence of attitudinal development. Worshiping God through true repentance for sin and an attitudinal expression of love for God in our worship is what He desires most.

Growth in the Area of Spiritual Action

The third area of spiritual development is in the volitional or active realm—the area of Christian living. The apostle John said,

> This is how we know what love is: Jesus Christ laid down his life for us. And we ought to lay down our lives for our brothers. If anyone has material possessions and sees his brother in need but has no pity on him, how can the love of God be in him? Dear children, let us not love with words or tongue but with actions and in truth (1 John 3:16–18).

Spiritual maturity in the area of the will involves obeying God, particularly by showing love to others. If we know what the Bible says but do not do what it instructs us to do, we are just hypocrites. There are several aspects of growth in the volitional realm, including changed behavior, social action, cooperation, and self-esteem. Our spiritual lives are characterized by the things we do as individuals and the things we do as a people. How that is expressed changes and grows with each stage of development. But we need to keep in mind that our students learn more about Christian living by *how* we teach than by *what* we teach. In cognitive spiritual development, teachers challenge the intellect with biblical facts and reasoning, but in volitional spiritual development, we go beyond teaching mere facts and show our students how to live godly lives by the way we live. Teaching methods include acting out godly behavior and including our students in planning acts of Christian love.

PRIMARIES GROW IN ALL THREE AREAS OF SPIRITUAL DEVELOPMENT

Each area of spiritual development has its own methods and objectives, depending upon the age group. First let's explore how primaries develop in each of these areas. See Figure 4 at the end of this chapter for more details.

Development of Spiritual Knowledge

Primaries learn all the things that preschoolers learn, but at a deeper level. At this stage, however, they are ready to be introduced to the way of salvation. Somewhere between the ages of 6 and 8, many children are able to understand in an elementary way that they have sinned and that Jesus died on the cross to take the punishment for their sins. They are also able to feel sorry for their sins and ask Jesus to save them.

Here is a summary of biblical truths that primaries can learn in the cognitive realm:

- God wants us to obey Him.
- The Bible tells us what God wants us to do.
- Jesus loves us.
- Jesus came to be our Savior.
- Jesus is with us.
- Jesus takes care of us.

Development of Spiritual Attitude

The African American church is unique in its celebrative style of worship. People love this kind of music because it touches their hearts. Teaching primaries to love Jesus is most effective through the avenues of the spirit and the emotions, because love is learning that takes place in the heart. Music is one of the most powerful ways to reach a child's spirit and emotions. We all know that the music many children listen to on the radio and on other media contain words that often shock us when we stop to really listen to them. But in the African American church, we have a great treasure of beautiful music with wonderful words that lift up Christ. When we sing these words, they enter into our being to touch our hearts in ways that mere spoken or written words cannot accomplish. Music is a gift from God, and African American church music is a special gift to all of us. Teachers can go beyond contemporary gospel songs to the old spirituals, chants, meter songs, and hymns to fill the hearts of primaries with a desire to worship the Lord in music. We can also teach biblical truth through the musical forms to which children can relate to today. For instance, a snappy Christian rap that teaches students the books of the Bible or other truths will stay in their minds as well as their hearts far better—and longer—than something they simply learned by rote.

In our classes we can help primaries learn to worship the Lord through songs, hymns, and spirituals. Children can also learn to compose simple tunes and raps as they think on the things they have learned. Other artistic expressions are also an effective means of educating the heart. Creative art, drama in the form of simple skits, and even dance can be used to worship the Lord. Bible stories and life application stories can be acted out to make the feelings of the characters the feelings of your primaries.

Building self-esteem is another important aspect of spiritual attitude because it equips primaries with the armor they need for life in a racist system. Our foundation for this self-esteem is the Bible. The psalmist wrote, "I praise you because I am fearfully and wonderfully made" (from Psalm 139:14). In the Old Testament we read, "So God created man in his own image, in the image of God he created him; male and female he created them" (Genesis 1:27). Moreover, in the grandest gesture of all, God sent His Son to die on the cross for us sinners—sinners who are of immeasurable worth to Him.

Building self-esteem in primaries begins with the sense of security we have in knowing that God created us, that He loves us, and that He sent His Son to die for us. But we also need to make a special effort to help African American primaries see themselves as beautiful in God's sight. We do this by showing them pictures in curriculum materials of children just like them; by using illustrations from the Bible that African American children can identify with and that reflect the African context; and by telling stories of African American heroes, especially those who are Christians. When we use these illustrations, it is often unimportant to mention to primaries that these people are Black. And that is not the real point anyway. The point is that African American children and African American people of all ages are God's beautiful creations, living for Jesus. Such education is stronger when "caught" than "taught."

Development of Spiritual Action

The first aspect of growth in the volitional or action realm is changed behavior. Progress in this area is easy to measure because we are looking for changes in what children do. We know that we can recognize Christians by their fruit (Matthew 7:16–20), so we can say that God has authorized us as "fruit inspectors." For primaries, that means living like Jesus. Among the actions that we will be looking for are doing good to others, helping in the community, witnessing about Jesus, and attending church.

Living in Christian community is an important part of spiritual growth in the volitional or action realm. The Bible compares the church to a body with eyes, hands, feet, nose, ears, and so forth (1 Corinthians 12:12–31).

The parts of the body do not compete against one another; they cooperate with one another. The gifts of each individual in the church are used to build up the body. We want primaries to grow in participation in that community. An important part of that participation takes place in Sunday School and in other Christian-education programs in the church. In this setting primaries learn that they are part of the church. Christian-education directors should look for opportunities to involve the children in as many aspects of the church as they can. Special thought and care need to be put into this so that participation will be meaningful for children in this developmental stage. We are all familiar with the church programs children participate in at Christmas and Easter, but children can also participate in church worship and in other kinds of presentations on a much more regular basis. Children's choirs are a great way to include the children in the life of the church, but they can also do skits and other presentations that demonstrate the things they are learning in Sunday School. If children are regularly present during worship services, the song leader can include songs that children enjoy and can relate to, the pastor can direct portions of his sermon to the children, and children can sometimes be given some special responsibilities, such as distributing hymnbooks and passing the offering plates.

Many African American Sunday Schools have opening and/or closing assemblies every Sunday morning. This is a very special time for children to demonstrate the things they are learning. They can recite their memory verses and give summaries of the Scripture passage upon which the lesson is based. These exercises are especially significant if they include the entire church, including the adults, because these community-in-learning times create "church" as it is meant to be.

In order to help primaries become functioning members of the body of Christ, we need to view the Sunday School class and other children's ministry classes as subsets of the church. One very important aspect of living in Christian community is the ability to cooperate with one another. Thus, we need Sunday School curriculum that emphasizes learning as a group and helping one another with classroom assignments rather than competing with one another. For instance, since primaries do not like to lose and tend to be poor competitors, we can teach them to work cooperatively with one another. Working together on projects is a good way to learn this skill. It is far better if children begin learning early in their development to cooperate with others in their activities so that they will continue to do so as adults.

JUNIORS GROW IN ALL THREE AREAS OF SPIRITUAL DEVELOPMENT

At each stage of development, children are learning new things and growing in new ways, but we assume that they are building upon a foundation of those things they have already learned. Therefore, it is necessary to continually review. When we stop to review earlier learning, some students are reflecting on what they learned in the previous stage of development, but they are rearranging these things in the context of more advanced understanding. Other students are learning spiritual truths, attitudes, and actions for the first time. However, because they are older than primaries, they can skip some of the initial learning and go right on to age-appropriate learning.

At each stage, children should be challenged to commit their lives to Christ in a way that is appropriate for their age. Even children who are born again at a younger age should be ready to promise to obey Christ, no matter how difficult that may be. When primaries accept Jesus as Savior, their ability to obey Him is typically limited to individual actions. But when juniors accept Christ, they can be challenged to commit to obeying Him as a way of life. See Figure 5 at the end of this chapter for more details.

Development of Spiritual Knowledge

The junior years are an even better time than the primary years for children to understand the way of salvation and to be born again. They can understand that God has rules and that they have disobeyed them. So if juniors have not yet accepted Christ as Savior, this age is a wonderful time for them to make that decision. Juniors can memorize Bible verses that describe the steps necessary for being saved or born again, and we can trust Scripture to convict their hearts.

Many juniors are able to commit longer passages of Scripture to memory. Because juniors are so adept at memorization, teachers may be tempted to skip checking their comprehension, but this is very important. If we do not teach children the meaning of what they are learning, we risk teaching them that the Bible is incomprehensible and irrelevant. Many juniors can be motivated to memorize Scripture through competition, but it is better to encourage students to learn together.

Juniors who have participated in Sunday School and other children's ministries since their early childhood may have a great store of knowledge of Bible stories. At this stage they begin to develop the ability to understand time and sequence and are ready to discover where these stories fit into the Bible. Juniors are also developing Bible study skills as they learn the books and divisions of the Bible, how to find things in the Bible, and how to read the Bible. Teachers need to go beyond questions that ask for simple repetition of what has been taught and focus on helping juniors learn how to understand the Bible for themselves.

Development of Spiritual Attitude

Juniors can learn to appreciate spirituals, gospel music, and a diversity of Christian music. Some enjoy worshiping God in the youth choir; others develop their own talents in worshiping the Lord through art, drama, writing, and other creative forms. As we offer juniors opportunities to try out different forms of expression, they will discover the gifts God has given them. Helping children discover their gifts is an important part of the job description for those who teach children in church ministry.

Juniors can also develop spiritually by starting their own personal Bible study habits. This is one of many areas of spiritual development that are not confined to one area of the spiritual-development triangle. By reading the Bible for themselves, juniors are learning biblical content, but even more important, they are developing habits that will lead to personal devotion to our Lord and to a deeper relationship with God that can impact their emotions and attitudes. As an additional benefit, the Bible has the power to show us how God wants us to live.

Teachers can suggest passages and stories from the Bible that are easy and enjoyable for juniors to read and understand. Teachers can also show juniors how to record their daily devotions on charts and logs. These are helpful aids for getting juniors into the habit of setting aside time each day for devotions. Beyond reading the Bible, teachers can help juniors learn how to pray. Prayer is the most important expression of the heart for someone who is learning to love and obey God. Teach your juniors to write prayer requests and praises in little notebooks. But even more, as you pray during class, your students will learn how to address God and what to speak to Him about. Your own spiritual attitude will be the most important means of teaching your children to love and honor God in conversation with Him.

Juniors are also looking for heroes, so this is a great time to acquaint them with Black heroes from all eras, including those from the Bible, such as Simon of Cyrene, Ebed-Melech, and others. African American Sunday School teachers and other church leaders are also important role models for juniors. For children who do not have father figures in their homes, it is especially important for teachers to point students to African American Christian males who are godly role models.

Development of Spiritual Action

Juniors are developing in the area of volition or action in ways that can be measured by behavioral objectives. Juniors can follow Christ by participating in community projects, such as neighborhood food drives. They can demonstrate love to individuals, such as friends and family members, in a variety of ways. They can also develop faithful attendance at church for Sunday School, worship services, children's clubs, and other activities of the church.

Juniors are also learning to live in community. Living in Christian community is even more important for juniors than for primaries. Primaries adore their teachers, but juniors seek to be admired by their peers. This can be a dangerous stage of development because some juniors are drawn to peers who may lead them in the wrong direction. But if we structure our Sunday School classes and church clubs as places where juniors can experience Christian fellowship and camaraderie, juniors will learn what it means to become a true part of the church family. Juniors are competitive, but if they lose, they have great trouble with self-confidence. So cooperative learning is still the best approach for meeting their needs. Since juniors enjoy the socialization of groups and clubs, teachers can foster a community of care and acceptance in the Sunday School class that will offer juniors an alternative to hanging out with the wrong crowd.

Conclusion

We want our students to progress holistically in the three realms of spiritual growth—knowledge, attitude, and action. By keeping in mind all three areas, their specific characteristics, and what kinds of growth we can expect in each area for primary-age and junior-age children, we can then tailor our teaching approach to meet the unique needs of each age group as we endeavor to lead each student to completion in Christ.

AREAS OF SPIRITUAL GROWTH

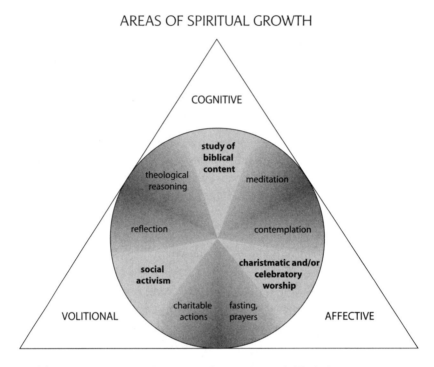

Figure 3. This triangle represents three areas of spiritual growth. The lighter sections represent most strongly and respectively the cognitive, affective, and volitional realms of spiritual development. Moving from any one area of the triangle toward another area indicates that growth in these areas has become more integrated or connected. The well-rounded Christian will demonstrate growth in all three areas.

WHOLE-LIFE
SPIRITUAL GROWTH

		Spiritual Development of Primaries
Knowledge		Learning about the way of salvation through the following truths: • God wants us to obey Him. • The Bible tells us what God wants us to do. • Jesus loves us. • Jesus came to be our Savior. • Jesus is with us. • Jesus takes care of us.
Attitude		Learning to worship the Lord through the following expressive forms: • Celebrative worship that includes contemporary and traditional African American songs and styles • Creative art, drama, and dance as a means to worship the Lord • Creative writing experiences on Bible stories and application stories • Building self-esteem through educational visuals and stories about African American heroes: • Pictures of children just like them • Realistic Bible characters with which African American children can identify
Action		Following Christ in the things they do: • Participating in community projects • Demonstrating love to others • Developing faithful attendance and participation in church activities Learning to work together through these cooperative activities: • Working together on group projects • Helping one another with classroom assignments • Helping family and friends

Figure 4. Whole-Life Spiritual Growth for Primaries

WHOLE-LIFE
SPIRITUAL GROWTH

	Spiritual Development of Juniors
Knowledge	Developing Bible skills by: • Memorizing Scripture passages and verses and learning to understand what they are memorizing. • Learning the books and divisions of the Bible, how to read the Bible, how to find things in the Bible, and how to place Bible stories and events in sequence. • Learning to think beyond just memorizing Bible verses and facts to understand the Bible for themselves by applying, analyzing, synthesizing, and evaluating.
Attitude	Experiencing group worship by: • Developing an appreciation for spirituals, gospel music, and a variety of Christian music. • Worshiping God in youth choir. • Developing individual talents to worship the Lord through music, art, drama, writing, and other creative forms. Developing individual Bible study and prayer habits through: • Reading the Bible for themselves so that they will grow in personal devotion for the Lord. • Learning to set aside time each day for devotions with the help of charts and logs. • Learning how to talk to God in prayer. • Keeping a journal of prayer requests and praises. Identifying with the following kinds of Black heroes and role models: • Afro-Semitic Bible characters in visual aids; Black heroes from Bible times and other historical eras. • African American teachers and leaders in the church. • African American Christian males who are godly role models for students without father figures in the home.
Action	Learning to live in Christian community through: • Cooperating with others. • Participating in Sunday School and church activities where they can experience a community of care and acceptance as an alternative to gangs or other negative group affiliations.

Figure 5. Whole-Life Spiritual Growth for Juniors

PART II:

USING AFRICAN AMERICAN TEACHING STYLES

CHAPTER 4

THE HISTORY OF BLACK CHURCH MINISTRY TO CHILDREN

In 1780 many poor children in England did not attend school; instead, they worked in factories six days a week. Sundays were the only day each week when they were free from their labors. They had no time to learn to read or write on the days they worked, and when they had a day off, they often got into trouble because they were unsupervised. On those days they tended to band together and destroy property. So Robert Raikes decided to start a school on Sundays to teach the children proper manners, personal hygiene, how to read, and how to live godly lives. He often bought food and clothes for the children, brought them to church with him, and even combed their hair.

THE FIRST AFRICAN AMERICAN SUNDAY SCHOOLS

Just a few years after Raikes established the first Sunday School, records show that White Methodists in the United States were interested in starting Sunday Schools for poor children, both Black and White. A plan was implemented to produce an instruction book from which to teach them. The American Methodists' vision and objectives for Sunday School were the same as Raikes'. They believed that Sunday School should encompass religious education as well as the teaching of reading and other skills needed for daily living.

Even in the early days of Sunday School in the United States, resistance arose against Christian education for Black children. George Daughaday of Charleston, South Carolina, was drenched with water from a public cistern "for the crime of conducting a Sunday School for the benefit of the African children of that vicinity" (Tyms 1979, 118).

The Baptists followed soon after the Methodists in establishing Sunday Schools. Around 1797 in Pawtucket, Rhode Island, a miller named Samuel Slater organized what is thought to have been the first Baptist Sunday School in the United States. Since the records state that the Sunday School was for poor free children (Tyms 1979, 105), it can be assumed that it at least included *free* Black children.

So from these old records we can see that Sunday School was established to provide not only spiritual education but also education in reading and other life skills by creating a curriculum that was designed to develop the whole person. We can also see that African Americans were among the first to participate in the Sunday School movement in the United States.

African American Sunday Schools in the Antebellum South

Although Southerners often used Scripture to justify slavery, they also recognized the fact that Jesus died for all—Black or White, slave or free—and they knew they had a duty to see that their slaves heard the Gospel. Almost all slave children were taught the Ten Commandments at an early age (Sernett 1975, 68).

Many slave owners thought that the Bible "properly taught" would make their slaves more honest and obedient, but slave owners were leery about Blacks reading the Bible for themselves, lest they read the whole Gospel and understand the truth about slavery and what the Bible taught about freedom and the worth of all human beings.

White Christians often provided Sunday School classes for Blacks in the South prior to the Civil War, but plantation owners limited what could be taught to the slaves. The whole of Scripture was not taught, and what was taught was twisted to serve the masters; that is, slaves were taught only to work hard and be obedient to their masters.

Reading Prohibited in African American Sunday Schools

Although the earliest Sunday Schools for African Americans included the teaching of reading, Southern Whites began to create a variety of ways to limit what was preached to Blacks, especially to slaves. Even though they saw their responsibility for sharing the Gospel with Blacks, they outlawed the teaching of reading to slaves because they did not want them to see the connection between the Christian faith as taught in the Bible and the principles of equality and freedom.

Nat Turner, who led a slave revolt, had learned to read in Sunday School. Furthermore, the reasons he gave for his actions were primarily religious (Sernett 1975, 46; Reed and Prevost 1993, 262). At his trial Turner asserted that "the Saviour [is] about to lay down the yoke he [bore] for the sins of men, and the great day of judgment [is] at hand" (Aptheker 1969, 123). Turner led a revolt in 1831 in which 61 White people were killed. The White community reacted even more violently by killing more than 100 Blacks (Fitts 1985, 61).

Denmark Vesey led a revolt of slaves in Charleston, South Carolina, in 1822. Two of the conspirators were Sunday School class members, and several witnesses implicated Morris Brown, a church pastor (Raboteau 1978, 163). At the trial of Vesey and his fellow conspirators, the court report mentioned that some of the accused were members of the Episcopal Church. They were said to have plotted the revolt during the class meetings of the local branch in Charleston (Sernett 1975, 38–39). And one witness reported that Vesey "read to us from the Bible, how the Children of Israel were delivered out of Egypt from bondage" (Aptheker 1969, 76). Slave revolts such as those led by Denmark Vesey and Nat Turner prompted southern states to make it illegal to teach slaves to read. Furthermore, religious services conducted by Blacks were banned. Thus, Christian education for Blacks was largely confined to oral teaching by White ministers and missionaries.

It was not easy for White missionaries to minister to Black slaves. They first had to obtain permission from the White slave owners. Obviously this placed constraints on what could be taught and how it was to be taught. Although some of the missionaries were less than enthusiastic about preaching that slaves had a duty to obey their masters, they were often compelled to do so in order to receive permission to preach and teach. The greatest handicap in the education of Blacks was a ban on the use of written materials for the religious instruction of slaves. By 1855, 9 of the 15 slave states had made it illegal to distribute Bibles among slaves (Sernett 1975, 65).

The fears of the slave owners were essentially well founded. They knew instinctively that any attempt to educate or indoctrinate their workers in biblical teachings would, in the long run, change the precarious relationship between master and slave. For this reason, many slave owners opposed any kind of religious instruction, preferring to maintain law and order by brute force rather than by a "paternalistic Christian education" (Wilmore 1984, 25).

Some Christians, especially Black Christians, did take a more active stance against slavery. On January 1, 1813, the New England Anti-Slavery Society was established and held its first meeting in a classroom of the African Church in Boston, Massachusetts (Sobel 1979, 257). And so, although Sunday Schools were not directly involved in combating slavery, they made a significant contribution to the anti-slavery movement by teaching literacy skills and preaching the truths of God's Word to Blacks.

Oral Instruction in African American Sunday Schools

Although many Northerners felt that religious instruction would fail without written materials, some White missionaries thought it would work because they had observed the oral traditions of the African slaves and knew of their remarkable memories. A variety of catechisms were used in teaching Blacks. Some catechisms were designed specifically for use in oral religious education while others were not. For instance, the catechism Isaac Watts used was designed for very young children and could be adapted for teaching illiterate slaves. Although the African heritage of passing on teaching through oral recitation made it possible for African Americans to receive a religious education, the problem was that oral catechisms were often designed by those who applied their own self-serving interpretations of God's Word. The ways in which the Gospel message was twisted can be seen in some of the questions and answers in the catechism: "What did God make you for?" "To make a crop." "What is the meaning of 'Thou shalt not commit adultery'?" "To serve our heavenly Father and our earthly master, obey our overseer, and not steal anything" (West 1893).

Eventually the Methodist, Baptist, and Presbyterian denominations split over the issue of slavery. Criticism of Southern slaveholders by Northern abolitionists prompted some Southerners to become more sensitive to their duty to provide religious instruction for their slaves, because one of the defenses of slavery as an institution was that it spread Christianity to Africans. So in spite of prohibitions against teaching slaves to read, Sunday School was held on many Southern plantations. These schools were organized for both children and adults, and all the instruction was oral. First, the teacher would ask questions and state the answers. Then the students would repeat both the questions and the answers until they had memorized the material. After that, the teacher would ask each student to answer a question.

Leadership in African American Sunday Schools

The historical records regarding Black Sunday Schools are scant, but they do at least give a superficial sense of what was happening during the early to mid-1800s. One written record reveals that in 1825 the first Black Sunday School was started by the First African Church of Savannah, Georgia. This tells us that African Americans were actively involved in establishing their own Sunday Schools at least as early as 1825. Many Black churches directed their own Sunday Schools in the North. However, Black-led Sunday Schools in the South were rare because of all the prohibitions placed on Blacks, both in assembling together for worship and in learning to read and write. More frequently, Black churches in the North had greater control of their own churches and Sunday Schools.

In 1850, the Fugitive Slave Act was implemented. According to this law, any slave who fled to the North for freedom could be captured and returned to his or her owner. This caused many church members to flee to Canada. But in spite of these losses, many Black churches and their Sunday Schools continued on with the help of God.

Black Sunday Schools During the Reconstruction Era

During the Civil War, many things came to a standstill. A small number of Sunday Schools in the South continued, because a few guilt-driven Whites excused slavery as an institution that introduced Christianity to Africans. African American-led Sunday Schools in the North continued advocating the abolition of slavery and providing a refuge in Christ during turbulent times.

After the Civil War, hundreds of Bible and Christian-book salesmen and missionaries, both Black and White, traveled around the South organizing Sunday Schools, even where there were no churches to support them (McCall 1986, 60–61). The Sunday Schools were held in homes as well as in churches and included a large number of Black laity. Quite often this effort was coordinated by the International Sunday School Association (Mitchell 1986, 107).

The International Sunday School Association and Northern denominations sought to train African Americans to teach Sunday School effectively in their own churches. Church-sponsored colleges often held model Sunday School classes before Sunday morning chapel in the hope that students would emulate this model and go out trained and committed to teach in African American Sunday Schools. Unfortunately, these colleges did not emphasize the importance of making the teaching culturally relevant, and so the students who used this model in their home churches found that they were not accepted by church leaders (McCall 1986, 61). The students had been trained in methods that were developed by White Christian educators who did not understand that lessons should begin where students are and that teachers should instruct students using methods that mesh with their unique learning styles.

When the Emancipation Proclamation took effect in 1863, African Americans eagerly sought formal education. At this time formal education was often fused or blended with oral traditional forms of instruction. Rope skipping, marching, and other rhythm games were often accompanied by counting, singing out the letters of the alphabet, or naming the states of the Union (Mitchell 1986, 105).

Sunday Schools were often the primary means of literacy instruction during the Reconstruction Era, which has been called the Golden Age of the African American Sunday School (Mitchell 1986, 112). With increased religious-education opportunities, African Americans began to mimic the patterns they saw in White Sunday Schools (Mitchell 1986, 106) and to rely on a curriculum provided by White organizations.

THE DEVELOPMENT OF AFRICAN AMERICAN SUNDAY SCHOOL CURRICULUM

The most significant event in the history of African American Sunday Schools after the Reconstruction Era was the development in 1896 of Sunday School curriculum by R. H. Boyd, a Black Baptist preacher and entrepreneur. Before the establishment of African American Baptist publishing boards, White Baptists often supplied religious curriculums to Black Baptists (Tyms 1979, 120–121), and they resented the publishing activities of Black Baptists (Moberg 1984, 449). When R. H. Boyd began his Sunday School publishing business, the American Baptist

Publications Society, who had been publishing a few articles by Black Christians, began refusing articles by African Americans. This decision gave further impetus to Black Baptists to produce their own literature, and within two years of the founding of R. H. Boyd's company, it became the largest African American publishing enterprise in the world (Fitts 1985, 82).

One pattern that was established early on in the use of printed Sunday School curriculum by African Americans was structuring lessons to follow the outlines of the Committee on the Uniform Series. The National Council of Churches of Christ in the U.S.A. is now the official producer of the outlines. The council publishes an outline for each year from September through August and divides it into quarters. Each outline includes a quarterly theme based upon a book of the Bible or another selection of Scripture passages along with weekly subthemes. The outlines follow a six-year cycle that covers every section of the Bible during that time. The individual Sunday School curriculum publishers pay royalties to subscribe to these outlines, and they base their lessons on the preselected Scripture passages.

Although the majority of White publishers have discarded the Uniform Lesson Series structure, most African American Sunday Schools still prefer it. There are many advantages to this approach. Pastors are able to refer to the Scripture passage in the outline and know that everyone in their congregation has been studying the same Scripture. Superintendents may plan Sunday School closing exercises around the weekly Sunday School theme as well as plan review activities that include every class. Parents may talk with their children about their Sunday School lessons and know what their children are studying in their classes. All of this creates unity in learning.

This style of curriculum development also forms an atmosphere in which all students, whether children or adults, feel that as a part of the church community, they must come to church prepared for the lesson, since the community conversation will be centered around it. If a teacher is absent, the superintendent knows that other adults have studied the Scripture passage and can teach the class. The chief drawback to the outline structure is that the Bible passages chosen are often difficult to teach to younger children because the selected Scripture passages are not always appropriate for this age group.

A Study of African American Sunday Schools in the 1940s

In 1945 St. Clair Drake and Horace R. Cayton published a milestone book, *Black Metropolis: A Study of Negro Life in a Northern City*, about a sociological study they conducted on Black life in Chicago. Their research showed that the African American church was an important part of the community. Of the 300,000 African Americans living in Chicago at that time, 65,000 attended church on Sunday, and among those who did not, many sent their children to Sunday School as a part of their "right raising" (Drake and Cayton 1945, 416). Drake and Cayton estimated that an average of 60,000 African American children attended Sunday School in Chicago in 1945. In storefront churches, everyone gathered together for two hours of singing, studying the lesson, and collecting the offering. In larger churches the students had their classes in separate classrooms with teachers who usually had certificates from the Interdenominational Council of Religious Education. In addition to Bible study, the lessons included a discussion of current events, race problems, and other issues.

Sunday Schools, even in storefront churches, also provided leadership training. Sometimes very small children gave reports to the entire church about what they were learning in Sunday School, while the older people looked on with approval and the superintendent and pastor gave them loud verbal encouragement (Drake and Cayton 1945, 628). The ability to give oral presentations in church was encouraged and affirmed by everyone.

African American Sunday Schools Today

A more recent study of African American churches, conducted through personal interviews and visits, was published in 1990 by C. Eric Lincoln and Lawrence H. Mamiya in their book *The Black Church in the African American Experience*. They noted that the vast majority of urban African American churches have Sunday School programs for both adults and children. They also found that churches in the South had very active Sunday School classes for adults. In the North, however, many Sunday School programs were quite small, with 10 to 20 adults and 25 to 50 children, depending on the size of the church. Lincoln and Mamiya blamed this on the pastors, who were not giving Sunday School programs the level of attention and leadership they needed. The study also found that many Sunday School classes seemed to exist primarily for babysitting purposes, and a number of churches put youth of all ages in one department (Lincoln and Mamiya 1990, 142).

However, despite the inadequacies of the Sunday School program in many African American churches, Sunday School is very important in the lives of African American youth. Lincoln and Mamiya concluded that African American Sunday Schools are second only in importance to the preaching in African American churches (Lincoln and Mamiya 1990, 105).

John Scanzoni, a University of Florida sociologist, found that the third most important role model for African American children is the Sunday School teacher. The minister ranked second and the public school teacher was first (Scanzoni 1971, 117).

The Christian-education programs of the Black church have made many contributions to the African American community. Sunday School teachers have helped children develop a healthy self-esteem and grow in their knowledge of the Bible through memorization and other learning methods. Churches have also equipped children and adults to assume leadership roles in the church, especially as Sunday School superintendents, and in the greater community.

However, Sunday School programs in the African American church have some weaknesses too. Perhaps the biggest weakness has been the tendency to cling to teaching patterns of the past without a healthy evaluation of these methods. Emmanuel L. McCall, author of *Black Church Life-Styles,* published in 1986, pointed to the pattern of having short classes preceded or followed by long assemblies. This dates back to the days when Black churches did not have Christian-education buildings, as many large churches do today. Formerly, everyone met in one large room, with a lengthy church assembly either preceding or following a short time for Sunday School. During Sunday School, students were separated into various classes according to age. However, since they were all in the same room, they could see everyone else and even hear some of what the other classes were learning. This, along with the larger assemblies, created a more communal style of learning. Teachers, who were largely untrained, found that shorter Sunday School classes worked best in this context. Today's Sunday School teachers often have their own classrooms, and they may be called upon to teach for longer periods of time partially because churches have to justify the building costs. As a result, churches may lose a feeling of community, and the inadequacies of some teachers' training and abilities may become more obvious.

African American Sunday School Curriculum Today

From the beginning, African American Sunday School literature has emphasized godly character, right conduct, spiritual regeneration, love, holiness, and righteousness, along with an obligation to God and humankind. Adherence to the teachings of the Bible has always been a central focus of the curriculum, regardless of the methods used (Tyms 1979, 205).

In the 1960s Melvin Banks Sr., Litt.D., worked for Scripture Press Publications, marketing their Sunday School curriculum to the African American community. Scripture Press, a White-owned and directed company, used illustrations in its curriculum that were based entirely on a White perspective of the Bible. Melvin Banks encouraged Scripture Press to include a small number of illustrations of African Americans in its curriculum, but many White churches, especially those in the South, said that if Scripture Press did this, they would no longer buy the curriculum.

Then in 1970, Scripture Press decided to underwrite the development of a new interdenominational Sunday School curriculum publishing company that would be owned and operated by African Americans for African Americans. The company was named Urban Ministries, Inc., and Melvin Banks was the founder as well as the president for the first 25 years. Mr. Banks led the movement away from mainstream Sunday School curriculum publishing toward producing a more culturally relevant curriculum for the African American community. Urban Ministries, Inc., had a more sophisticated, commercial style of art than other curriculum publishers, and the company soon began to make a dent in both the markets of the African American denominational publishers and the White publishers who produced curriculum for the African American community.

In 1975 Urban Ministries, Inc. introduced Bible illustrations with its curriculum. The company wanted to use biblical visual aids that African Americans could relate to and that would be more historically and culturally accurate than the illustrations used in White publications. In his introduction to William Mosely's book, *What Color was Jesus?*, Jeremiah A. Wright Jr. asserts the fact that much of the religious art in the Western world has been strongly influenced by the art of the Italian Renaissance in which painters used their own people as models for their work (Mosely 1987, viii). The invention of the printing press spread these illustrations all over the world, and Anglo-Saxons in the United States have contributed their own artistic interpretations, which has even further removed biblical characters from their geographic origins.

Urban Ministries, Inc. is not the first to portray biblical characters as dark-skinned people. In fact, one can find such illustrations all the way back when Bible art first appeared. The attempts of Blacks, Whites, Asians, or other ethnic groups to portray biblical characters as "one of us" indicates a heartfelt desire to apply Bible teaching to one's own context.

A number of Scriptures in the Old Testament indicate that Black people were present in the Bible, such as the wife of Moses, the Queen of Sheba, and the Ethiopian official. Israel is located at the crossroads of Asia, Africa, and Europe. Perhaps this tells us something about how God views the ethnicity of the people of the Bible. Urban Ministries, Inc. sees its Bible characters as representing a more North African, Semitic people than we usually see in Bible illustrations. Not only are these images more accurate historically and geographically, but they also provide African American children with positive Black images so they will develop an appreciation of their infinite worth in the eyes of God.

A further distinctive of Urban Ministries, Inc. curriculum is the inclusion of African American historical personalities in both the Sunday School and the Vacation Bible School curriculum. Paulo Freire, a Brazilian educator who spoke about the need for the liberation of oppressed people, said that curriculum must not treat people as unfortunates but must present them with role models of their own that will serve as examples for their redemption (Freire 1996, 36).

Although it continues to remain an innovator in publishing Christian education resources that are contextualized for African Americans, Urban Ministries, Inc. is not the only publisher of Sunday School curriculum for African Americans. David C. Cook, a Caucasian publishing house, publishes an imprint targeted for the African American audience. Since 1896, R. H. Boyd continues to publish Sunday School curriculum for the African American Baptist audience. Urban Ministries, Inc. is the only interdenominational Sunday School curriculum publisher that is African American owned and operated. Because of its strong commitment to contextualizing the biblical world view for African Americans, Urban Ministries, Inc. is by far the current leader in the field of publishing Sunday School curriculum for African Americans.

Reference List

Aptheker, Herbert, ed. *A Documentary History of the Negro People in the United States. Vol. 1, From Colonial Times Through the Civil War.* New York: Citadel Press, 1969.

Drake, St. Clair, and Horace R. Cayton. *Black Metropolis: A Study of Negro Life in a Northern City.* New York: Harcourt, Brace and Company, 1945.

Fitts, Leroy. *A History of Black Baptists.* Nashville: Broadman Press, 1985.

Frazier, E. Franklin. *The Negro Church in America.* New York: Schocken Books, 1966.

Freire, Paulo. *Pedagogy of the Oppressed.* Rev. ed. Translated by Myra Bergman Ramos. New York: Continuum, 1996.

Lincoln, C. Eric, and Lawrence H. Mamiya. *The Black Church in the African American Experience.* Durham, N.C.: Duke University Press, 1990.

McCall, Emmanuel L. *Black Church Life-Styles.* Nashville: Broadman Press, 1986.

Mitchell, Ella P. "Oral Tradition: Legacy of Faith for the Black Church." *Religious Education* 81 (Winter 1986): 986.

Moberg, David O. *The Church As a Social Institution.* Grand Rapids: Baker Book House, 1984.

Mosely, William. *What Color Was Jesus?* with an introduction by J. Wright Jr, Ph.D. Chicago: African American Images, 1987.

Raboteau, Albert J. *Slave Religion: The "Invisible Institution" in the Antebellum South.* New York: Oxford University Press, 1978.

Reed, James E., and Ronnie Prevost. *A History of Christian Education.* Nashville: Broadman and Holman, 1993.

Scanzoni, John H. *The Black Family in Modern Society.* Boston: Allyn and Bacon, 1971.

Sernett, Milton C. *Black Religion and American Evangelicalism*. White Protestants, Plantation Missions, and the Flowering of Negro Christianity, 1787–1865. Metuchen, N.J.: Scarecrow, 1975.

Sobel, Mechal. *Trabelin' On: The Slave Journey to an Afro-Baptist Faith*. Westport, Conn.: Greenwood, 1979.

Tyms, James D. *The Rise of Religious Education Among Negro Baptists*. Washington, D.C.: University Press of America, 1979.

West, Anson D. *A History of Methodism in Alabama*. Nashville: Publishing House, Methodist Episcopal Church, South, 1893.

Wilmore, Gayraud S. *Black Religion and Black Radicalism: An Interpretation of the Religious History of Afro-American People*. Maryknoll, N.Y.: Orbis Books, 1984.

CHAPTER 5

DISCOVERING AFRICAN AMERICAN TEACHING STYLES

During the fall of 1998, I studied the teaching styles of African American teachers of primary and junior students in the Sunday Schools of three large African American churches in the Chicago area (Hull 1999). One church belonged to a historic Black Baptist denomination and was located in the inner city. Another church, located on the outer fringes of the city, belonged to a predominantly White mainline denomination and drew from a variety of socioeconomic groups among both students and teachers. The third church was part of a historic Black Methodist denomination and was located in a wealthy suburb. The Sunday School teachers at this church were professional, middle-class and upper-middle-class individuals, and the students were from families of similar socioeconomic standing. Despite the diversity of the communities in which the three churches were located, the differences in the socioeconomic levels of their members, and the varied histories of the denominations to which they belonged, I observed several similarities in teaching styles. All three churches in the study were using the same curriculum. By minimizing differences in teaching styles based solely on the teaching strategies advocated by a particular Christian publishing company, I was able to draw data comparisons and make more meaningful observations. Although I studied the pedagogical approaches teachers used in Sunday School, these same approaches may be used in Vacation Bible School, weekday children's Bible clubs, and other Christian-education settings.

The data for this study was collected using several methods: observation of teachers as they taught their classes, interviews with those teachers after the class periods, interviews with Sunday School superintendents, and a study of the individual histories of the churches to understand the settings. The findings were presented descriptively; in other words, no numbers or statistics were involved. I spent one month in each church observing the educational strategies of the teachers in their classrooms and interviewing them afterward. I looked at such things as how the chairs were arranged in the class, how visual aids were utilized, what types of questions the teachers asked, what physical facilities were provided for the Sunday School program and what this revealed about the way each church viewed teaching, and so on. The interview questions were open-ended so that participating teachers could freely express their views of the learners and their evaluations of their teaching strategies. Often, comments that seemed to deviate from the prepared questions revealed more than the direct responses to those questions.

After completing the research, I spread out all the interviews and observation data and looked for patterns and clusters of educational strategies. Then from those patterns I looked for emerging themes. The following themes emerged from the data: (1) learning in community, (2) leadership through consensus building, (3) a transmissive approach to learning, (4) a dialogical style of teaching, and (5) a firm belief that Jesus Christ is the answer to the needs of the learners.

LEARNING IN COMMUNITY

The first theme I observed during my research was learning in community. This was the part of the research I enjoyed most. I first got acquainted with members of one church while sitting in the church cafeteria having a cup of coffee and a slice of potato pie. At another church I attended a one-day teachers' retreat in a lovely old mansion devoted to urban seminars and listened to the superintendent and teachers discuss their thoughts on disciplining children, sharing with beggars on the street, and gradually losing "moans," an old type of Black church music. And at the third church, I sat with a superintendent and his two little girls in the worship service every Sunday after Sunday School for a month. But most of all, I enjoyed sitting in on classes as the teachers related the Gospel and boys and girls responded enthusiastically.

There were many evidences of community-style learning in the three African American Sunday Schools in this study. Both of the Sunday Schools located within the large urban municipality had mechanisms for fostering theological unity. At the inner-city church, the teachers were required to attend weekly teachers' meetings for each department. The primary teachers met together as a group, the junior teachers met together, and so on. Each department superintendent conducted the meeting, which was primarily a Bible study on the material for the coming Sunday. Then the teachers and the department superintendent discussed how to present the material to their classes. These meetings established close fellowship within the departments and ensured that all the teachers were in accord on the meaning of the weekly Scripture passage. If the teachers could not reconcile their views of the lesson, then the Sunday School superintendent would make the final decision about the view that would be taught. During the interview the superintendent told me that he thought it was important for all the teachers to be "on the same page" and that he did not want everyone teaching something different. He also said that if they later discovered that they were in error on a particular issue, they would all correct the error together.

The church on the fringes of the city was less intentional about developing theological unity, but those on the Christian-education staff had obvious respect for their pastor and his theological viewpoints. They quoted him often, and he also mentored many of his church members and staff in theology. Several teachers spoke of "tweaking" the Sunday School curriculum to reflect the worldview of their pastor and their church. The teachers and those in leadership positions actively interpreted the theology of the community. They especially wanted the students to understand through the study of the Bible that they have a legacy to be proud of.

The chief means of developing a spiritually unified viewpoint in the Sunday School of this church was their annual one-day retreat. Each department was given a written curriculum for the retreat, with short meditations on several topics. We had breakfast and lunch together, sat around in comfortable clothes, listened to some traditional Black church music, and had an enriching time discussing all the items in the retreat curriculum.

In contrast to the urban churches, the suburban church did not seem to have any system of ensuring theological unity within the Sunday School program. The church had no regular Sunday School teachers' meetings, and everyone seemed to be too busy to attend meetings that were not scheduled on Sundays.

All three churches and their Sunday Schools may be viewed as extended families. The church on the fringes of the city was the most intentional in developing unity, as evidenced by their teachers' retreats. They also mentioned that new teachers and more experienced teachers worked together in the Sunday School as an extended family. The inner-city church was just as committed to the church functioning as an extended family, except that the people used the traditional biblical term *fellowship* to describe it.

Within the community-in-learning dynamic I also noticed evidence in all three churches of mentoring relationships, particularly in the ways teachers viewed their students. Mrs. Clark said that teachers need to give the children of this generation some guidance:

> With all the things that are going on in this world, children cannot grow up without knowing the Lord and having Him on their side. They need to know at an early age who they are and *whose* they are. This understanding does not come from reading a psychology book—it takes people giving their time to help young people develop as they should. Teachers need to bring children on to adulthood.
>
> The mentoring model works especially well with children because they obviously know so much less than adults do.

The three oldest teachers in this study underscored the importance of the mentoring dynamic when they told me they felt they had a responsibility to teach because they had received so much teaching themselves. One of the teachers, who was in her 60s, had just begun teaching Sunday School. While respect for the wisdom of age was most obvious in the two urban churches, this was not as apparent in the suburban church, where none of the teachers were older than sixty. As I looked out at the congregation on Sunday mornings, most of the members appeared to be young. Moving out to primarily White suburbs is a recent occurrence among African Americans, and it is mostly younger people who have made this move.

In all three churches, some teachers mentored other teachers who had less experience. Sometimes this was part of the program structure, and sometimes it was something that simply evolved. In one team-teaching situation, the older teacher had recruited the younger, but this relationship had not been imposed upon them by the Sunday School structure. Mrs. White told me how this came about. The younger woman, Ms. Young, saw Mrs. White waiting in a long line at the hospital. Ms. Young, who worked at the hospital, recognized Mrs. White as a fellow church member and brought her to the head of the line. This interaction began the relationship, and ever after, Mrs. White has called Ms. Young her godchild.

All of the churches used some form of team teaching, which is perhaps the most intensive kind of pedagogical community. In one church I observed two teachers in the junior department teaching the same class by alternating from one teaching segment to the next. This was done so seamlessly that I was surprised to find out that they had not planned ahead as to which teacher would teach which segment. They functioned almost as one.

At the church on the fringes of the city, each class had about four teachers whose teaching responsibilities varied. In one class each teacher was responsible for a different week. Although they were not all physically present each week for the teaching, they still needed a high level of coordination so they could keep the teaching flowing, stay involved with their students, and do some special things that individual teachers might be able to do especially well.

At the suburban church, two teachers took turns with the class, but they were such good friends that they talked on the phone every night and always knew what the other was doing. On the day I was scheduled to observe, one teacher was sick and the other was unexpectedly called upon to take her place. Because she knew exactly what the other teacher would have done, she was able to take over the teaching responsibilities without hesitation. Each teacher understood the teaching style of the other and appreciated what the other was able to do.

In the inner-city church, the teachers were flexible about which children they had in their classes. For instance, if more 8-year-olds showed up, some might be placed with the 7-year-olds. Rotation of teachers, or of those standing in for the regular teachers, took place at all three churches, and the children responded with grace whenever this happened. This seemed in keeping with the dynamics of extended families in which children might be shifted from grandmother to mother to father.

All three churches involved in this study were physically structured in ways that encouraged community. The inner-city church served dinner in their cafeteria every Sunday after church. This cafeteria was a natural place to gather before Sunday School. The smells of sweet potatoes, greens, and ham cooking could not fail to draw in people long before dinner. In fact, it was such a magnet that rules had to be made to ensure that teachers and students were in Sunday School during class time rather than just fellowshiping with one another. The 40-minute period between Sunday School and the morning worship service was also a time for many to gather in the cafeteria. The teachers often gathered there for a cup of coffee and a piece of pie or cake, and the children knew they could find their teachers there.

Two of the churches had large open areas for teaching rather than individual classrooms, which increased the feeling of community. The other church had individual classrooms for primaries, but a large open space for the juniors. Children and teachers in these undivided areas were in close proximity to one another, even when they were in different classes. Even in the church with dividers, the space was open at the beginning of Sunday School so that children and teachers could see one another as they arrived and got settled. In the churches that used large open teaching spaces, children and teachers could see their family members and friends in other classes across the room, which made them feel more connected to one another. Ms. Randolph told me she was given a separate space in the church computer room, but she wanted to return to teaching in the large open space. She said the computer room was too small, but I suspect that she really enjoyed being a part of the bustle in the large room upstairs with all the other primary and junior classes.

Several other factors in these churches pointed to the view that learning is a community activity. Even the way all of the churches handled discipline problems illustrates the emphasis placed on community. The teachers saw themselves as playing a role in the lives of their students, but not the *only* role. They were cognizant of the fact that others in the church were part of the process. In fact, many of the teachers mentioned talking with the parents of the children who exhibited behavior problems in the classroom. The first step in dealing with a behavior problem was to isolate a student from his or her peers. Then a teacher or superintendent would talk with the student. If that did not work, then the parents were brought into the process. This is another evidence of the church and all its members working together as an extended family to solve one another's problems.

All three churches in this study used Sunday School curriculum based on the Uniform Lesson Series. In this curriculum, all age levels study the same Scripture passage on a given Sunday. As I mentioned earlier, a much larger percentage of African American Sunday Schools prefer this format than do other Sunday

Schools. Although some Scripture passages are difficult to teach young children, the Uniform Lesson Series accommodates greater community involvement in learning. It also enables churches to center worship during opening or closing assemblies on the material all the students are learning. In addition, parents may talk at home with their children about the lessons. And if a teacher is absent, most of the adults in the church have studied the Scripture passage for their own class and can be expected to be able to teach the children when needed.

LEADERSHIP THROUGH CONSENSUS BUILDING

Two of the teachers in the primary department at the inner-city church told stories about how they ended up in that department. Mr. Wallace, the one male in the department, said that after he had finished the teacher-preparation course, he wanted to teach the teens or young adults. However, the superintendent told him there were no openings for teachers at that level. Consequently, the superintendent placed Mr. Wallace in the primary department, supposedly for a brief period. As Mr. Wallace taught the primary children, he realized that many of these children needed a godly male role model in their lives. They responded to him and he responded to them. As a result, this single young man decided to continue teaching the primaries. Even after he got married and had children of his own, he stayed in the primary department teaching young children.

Ms. Clinton, the department superintendent, had also gone through the teacher-training course and hoped to be placed in an adult class. She was a public school teacher and thought she saw enough of the children during the week. Again, the Sunday School superintendent said he wanted to place her "temporarily" in the primary department, but she also stayed for years in this position.

When Mr. Wallace and Ms. Clinton confided these stories to me, I was surprised by the way the superintendent seemed to manipulate them into teaching the primaries. But they both chuckled over the methods of the superintendent and said they were sure that they were in the classes God wanted them to be in.

Although all three Sunday Schools exhibited a style of teaching and learning that focused on community and partnership with one another, these programs also emphasized strong leadership. The previous example in which the superintendent placed the teachers in the primary department despite their initial reluctance to teach this age group reflects the power of that superintendent, the political machinations of his leadership, and the strongly hierarchical nature of his Sunday School. But the secret to this type of strong leadership was clearly his ability to build consensus. The superintendent was always working to bring about agreement or consensus with the teachers regarding his vision for the best way to direct the Sunday School.

At the church on the fringes of the city, the entire staff was anxious to develop a theology for the Sunday School that reflected their pastor's views. The members of the congregation obviously held their minister in very high regard. This gives a little clue as to the nature of the seeming contradiction between a heavy emphasis on group participation and a strong leadership structure. This type of community is not governed as a democracy, in which the majority rules and each member has a vote; nor is it a dictatorship. Leaders in these three African American churches and Sunday Schools led by consensus. Consensus building demands a great deal of time—time that is spent on relationship building and arguing for one's point of view. Much discussion is needed to bring about consensus and reach a decision, but greater unity is built in the process.

The seeming contradiction of pairing a communal approach to learning with a powerful leadership structure is resolved in the nature of the leadership. Those in leadership function only with the support of the community. A leader without the ability to bring about consensus is not a leader; thus, the highly political nature of the hierarchy. Leaders and all those in community are constantly working toward building support for the consensus. Leading the body requires much discussion. Particularly at the inner-city church, I could see the superintendent taking teachers aside to talk with them about various issues. His business was to bring along the entire staff so that everyone shared a common viewpoint.

In the suburban church, the leadership style of the superintendent was more nondirective. He had only been in the position for two years and so relied on the abilities of the Sunday School teaching staff. In this Sunday School, the teachers in each department got together and decided the objectives for their departments, but the criteria for graduation to the next department had been set by the previous superintendent.

Some teachers stressed obedience to parents, teachers, and pastors as a means of building respect for strong leaders in the church and in the home. Children were taught to show respect for those in positions of authority by learning from them and submitting to them.

Sunday School in all three churches began with prayer. Before their departmental devotions, the inner-city church always prayed while everyone stood in a circle and held hands. The church on the fringes of the city had individual classes, but each class held hands and prayed at the beginning. In the suburban church, the Sunday School superintendent began with prayer while every boy, girl, and teacher held hands in a gigantic circle. This was a very physical representation of the unity of the fellowship in all three churches. Although a teacher or superintendent usually led the prayer, the circle reminded everyone that the community was unified and that each member of the community had equal value. In other words, there was a leadership hierarchy, but relationships superceded the rules of the hierarchy.

The hierarchical structure of the Sunday Schools in the three churches varied greatly. The inner-city church had the most hierarchy, the church on the fringes of the city was much less hierarchical than the inner-city church, and the suburban church was the least hierarchical of the three. It also exhibited the least amount of politicking. However, regardless of the varied hierarchical structures, decision making was accomplished through consensus building in all churches.

A TRANSMISSIVE APPROACH TO LEARNING

In African American churches, Sunday School is serious business. There are important things to teach, and biblical content is at the heart of each lesson. Such a perspective leads to the transmissive approach to learning. This approach views education as the transferal of content from the teacher to the student. It also assumes that learning is primarily a cognitive activity. Biblical facts are the main focus of the Sunday School lesson. The primary teaching methods include telling the students the things the teacher thinks they should know, reading the week's lesson and Scripture passage to the students, and asking students questions about the facts of the lesson. The transmissive approach is primarily verbal; that is, it involves the use of words, either written or spoken. African American Sunday

School teachers are serious about God's Word, and they do a terrific job teaching children the content of the Bible.

The African American Sunday School teachers in this study demonstrated a great commitment to the content of the Bible, beginning with class preparation. They prepared for the lesson by studying the biblical content in great depth, but some did not read the teaching plan. These teachers obviously felt that the biblical content was much more important than the methods of instruction. This is the first characteristic of a transmissive approach to learning.

The importance of retention is another characteristic of the transmissive approach. All of the teachers emphasized reviewing the biblical content of the lessons, and many teachers talked about the importance of remembering past events and traditions in African American history. Miss Hall mentioned the importance of family reunions for remembering family histories. Generational memory is important to African Americans because it was often denied them by the White slavery system. Few African Americans are able to trace their ancestral history back to Africa. Generational memory is also important because long before Africans were captured and brought to this country, they traced their ancestral history back many generations. Remembering ancestors is a transmissive activity. In the past it was a hearing and reciting activity; today it is a reading and writing activity.

The African American Christians in this study found their history in the Bible in varying degrees. Mrs. White said that it was important for African American children to learn biblical history because it was *their* history. She viewed the Bible as a very African book.

A third characteristic of the transmissive approach is the structure of the curriculum. All three churches used curriculum that followed the Uniform Lesson Series. This was partly due to tradition, but there were other reasons these churches preferred a curriculum structure in which everyone was learning the same thing at the same time, regardless of age level. This indicates a focus on cognitive content, the main characteristic of a transmissive approach. One aspect of the curriculum that the churches liked is the six-year cycle, which covers a portion of each area of Scripture over this period of time. This spiral curriculum framework works very well with a transmissive approach to learning and teaching.

The structure of class schedules could also be interpreted as favoring the transmissive approach. Although the printed curriculum gave teachers a variety of ideas for getting the attention of the students at the beginning of class, the majority of the teachers in my study ignored these suggestions. At the inner-city church, each department started with devotions. The primary teachers structured their department devotions so the children would read the summary statements and the key verse associated with the lesson that was included with the publisher's curriculum. That would seem to make the Bible lesson rather anticlimactic, but this procedure underlines the teachers' commitment to teaching the content. It also underlines the seriousness with which the teachers viewed the spiritual message. They did not want to waste any time with anything that they did not think would contribute to learning the content.

Additional evidence of the transmissive approach could be seen in how the three churches motivated children to learn the content. All three Sunday School programs recognized the accomplishments of the children in formal promotion ceremonies. At the suburban church the primaries had to learn the Lord's Prayer, the Twenty-third Psalm, and the order of the first few books of the Bible before being promoted to the junior department. Some teachers even gave rewards to students for learning the transmitted content. For instance, Ms. Jones promised her students "fantastic prizes" for learning the Ten Commandments. The content was decided by the community; that is, the primary teachers got together and decided what they thought the primaries should learn, and the junior teachers got together to decide what the juniors should learn.

Although all the teachers concentrated on teaching the cognitive content of the Bible, they described the content in more relational terms. Teachers spoke of teaching their students to love one another. For instance, Ms. Blackwell described the things she strove to teach her primaries: "Don't fight with your friends at school and at church. Show respect for your church, your pastor, your mother, your father, and your teachers at school. Love is important." I will discuss in the next chapter whether the transmissive approach is best for teaching children about relationships.

Another important characteristic of the transmissive approach that I observed in the three churches was the involvement of the Sunday School in interpreting the content for the learners. Although the right to interpret the meaning of the content is not necessarily a component of the transmissive approach, in these three church-es it was very significant. All three decided to use, for the most part, a curriculum that was produced by African Americans for African Americans. They saw the im-portance of the African American church playing a primary role in making mean-ing of the lesson content for African American children, and almost all the teach-ers were enthusiastically involved in interpreting the content in their teaching. The diligent study of the Scripture passages in their teaching preparations, along with an almost complete exclusion of the teaching plan, underscores the point that these teachers felt they had a right to interpret the lesson content for their students.

A DIALOGICAL STYLE OF TEACHING

Mr. Jones said that when he taught his first Sunday School class, he used a sort of lecture style. He quickly told his students all the important points of the les-son, and within 15 minutes he was finished. That left three-quarters of an hour of class time yet to fill. But after he had taught for a few years, he found himself ask-ing lots of questions and interacting with his students. This method seemed more suitable to Mr. Jones, but where did such insight come from? Think of the call and response of African American church music. Think of the antiphonal style of the Black preacher and the congregation. Mr. Jones was using this same dialogical mode of teaching in his primary classroom.

Dialogue is a special kind of talk that affirms those on both sides of the discussion. It is also an important means of communicating the community's interpretation of biblical content. True dialogue acknowledges the intellectual capacity of the discussion participants and their right to make sense of their world. (Dixon 1996, 24–25). African American Sunday School teachers are in continuous interaction with their students through questions. The highly dialogical method I observed in all the classrooms was teaching in relationship. Mrs. White said during her inter-view that "talking is sharing and explaining ourselves." Dialogue leads to shared meaning (Dixon 1996, 12).

I observed that the form of instruction used to begin classes was often the form that teachers favored most. Although one teacher followed the suggestion in the lesson plan and used objects as an illustration to introduce the lesson, most of the teachers began with dialogue.

In the primary classes, especially, the most commonly asked question was, "What did I just say?" Although this may be the easiest type of question for primaries to answer, better questions can be asked that will contribute to higher levels of learning. More will be said in chapter 6 about the kinds of dialogue.

The dialogue in the Sunday School classes had a special vocabulary. Some critics say that clichés are overused in the Black church, and many educators would argue even more strongly that we must be careful to say things in a way that children can understand. But there is another side to this issue.

In my study I noticed that some teachers quoted phrases or titles from popular African American Christian music in explaining their ideas. Others even used titles from current African American movies. But most of all, teachers used terminology that came straight from the Bible. There is a unique language in African American churches to be learned and taught. That language is constantly changing, and yet it is historically based upon a shared heritage.

Just as African American children must learn one language to live within the African American community and another to succeed in the American mainstream, so they need to learn the language that is being taught in the Black church. This language is both biblical and African American. It is the language of African American Christians, steeped in the narratives and vocabulary of the Bible, the phrases of African American church music, the antiphonal structure of African American sermons, and the dialogical style of teaching. The dialogical style used so extensively by African American Sunday School teachers is a good method for teaching African American children this church language.

A FIRM BELIEF THAT
JESUS CHRIST IS THE ANSWER

When I was conducting my research, one Sunday morning in early September was especially warm. A noisy room air conditioner was chugging along next to a class of children in one of the very large open areas. One boy was fanning himself with his lesson folder. Sweat was streaming down the face of the teacher, who was wearing a very heavy wool suit with a brown handkerchief in the pocket and a matching necktie. The children's answers to the teacher's questions were barely audible above the air conditioner, and many of the children were staring out the window. Only the teacher's commitment and faith in Jesus Christ could keep him going, and only a deep trust in what God is able to do through the power of His Word could motivate parents to send their children to Sunday School under such difficult conditions.

Most of the teachers I interviewed referred to the fact that their students had great problems to face. Those in the two urban churches mentioned poverty, drugs, and dysfunctional families. The teachers said that the children were preoccupied with personal problems that impeded their learning. Their minds were also bombarded with negative images from the media. Because of the moral breakdown that these teachers witnessed in the world and in the African American community, they saw the value of teaching children at an early age what the Bible says. Moreover, they felt a moral responsibility to do so. Mr. Brown said, "The children need something to create values, ethics, and morals." The teachers saw the problem as a community problem requiring a community solution.

In an interview with Miss Washington, she said,

> The solution to many of the problems that the children face is loving them
> a lot and developing their trust. But ultimately, if we teach the children to
> truly love Jesus, everything else will fall in line. If they truly love Jesus,
> they will be obedient to the kingdom's constitution, which is the Bible.

She also said that if teachers will instill in their students a love of Jesus and His care for other people, they will not have so much shooting and killing in their communities. She tells her students, "It does not matter if you have any friends, because you have a friend in Jesus."

Teachers saw Jesus as both Savior and their example for living. Two teachers from the inner city said that the most important thing to teach is "how to accept Christ, so the children can be saved and so they can be witnesses." They also said that it is "important to teach them how to act Christlike." They wanted the children to love Jesus so much that they would want to do what He says. And they felt they must instill this in the children while they were young.

The teachers in the suburban church did not think that the problems their students faced were as difficult as those the children in the urban areas had to face.

But whatever problems the children were facing, the teachers firmly believed that Jesus Christ is the answer.

Reference List

Dixon, Nancy M. *Perspectives on Dialogue.* Greensboro, North Carolina: Center for Creative Leadership, 1996.

Hull, Judith St. Clair. "African American Sunday School Teachers' Views of the Learners and Teaching." Ann Arbor, Mich.: UMI Dissertation Services, 1999.

CHAPTER 6

UTILIZING THE BEST IN AFRICAN AMERICAN TEACHING STYLES

Now that we have an understanding of the themes that characterized the teaching styles of those I observed, we can utilize these themes to identify teaching methods that work well with African American children. One example of this is the teacher who taught his first class in 15 minutes instead of filling the hour allotted and then eventually developed a dialogical style of teaching using lots of questions and class participation. This teacher discovered an approach that worked well for both him and his students.

My hope is that by examining each of the teaching styles available to us, we will be able to determine which will work best for African American children. An honest critique of pedagogical methods can also make teaching in the African American church even more effective.

LEARNING IN COMMUNITY

Community is one of the greatest gifts God has given us. God Himself is a community of three-in-one. When Adam was first created, he was alone, and so God created the first human community—the community of marriage between Adam and Eve. From the beginning, the human community was originally designed for a unified language, but that unity was destroyed at the Tower of Babel. After Babel, people were divided into different groups or nations. God could have punished humankind by making each person an island to himself or herself, but instead He created communities of particular people groups. Therefore, the result of human pride and ambition was division, but even in that division, God gave the gift of community. (A description of the ancient community groups God created is presented in Genesis 10, the Table of Nations.)

Although God has always dealt with individuals, He also calls people groups to Himself. In the Old Testament God promised Abraham that He would bless all nations through him and would make him into a "great nation"—Israel—that God would set apart as His special people (Genesis 12:2–3; Leviticus 26:12). Jonah's commission to go to Nineveh is a particular example of how God spoke to nations through the prophets (Jonah 1:1).

In the New Testament, God called out another special people—the church. The church is made up of individuals from many nations, but the Lord did not lose His interest in groups of people. The apostle Luke, in particular, was very interested in the national and ethnic identity of people. All through Luke's gospel, the national origins of people are mentioned. In the book of Acts, Luke continued to write about God's concern for people as members of nations, such as when he listed the various groups of people present at Pentecost (see Acts 2:5–11). God's concern for groups of people is especially comforting to African Americans because African Americans have been discriminated against and oppressed as a people (Roberts 1987, 66).

The African American church has been the center of the Black community for more than two centuries and was God's gift to Black people when they had little else. The Black church has been a source of comfort and consolation in all of life's troubles, an extended family of Christian fellowship, a place for leadership development, and a unified body for social protest. Moreover, the Black Sunday School has been the chief context for learning in this community.

African American Christians practice community in learning no matter what the structure of the Sunday School. Team teaching in its many forms is a favorite teaching style in Black churches because it is an effective structure for learning in community, in which teachers also encourage children to help one another. Other teaching structures can also be used to promote learning in community. For instance, children can be paired off in learning teams or in other kinds of groupings to help one another learn the lesson material. No matter what teaching structures are currently being used in the Black church, teachers are helping African

American children grow up and mature in their faith so that they will become adult believers who function as a Christian learning community.

Dialogue is the means by which learning in community is able to take place. Paulo Freire envisions teachers and learners in community reversing their roles so that teachers see themselves as learners and learners see themselves as teachers (Freire 1996, 53). Although children are not on the same thinking level as adults, there is great value in teachers seeing themselves as learners along with the children. But this requires teachers to listen very carefully and imitate the ways children learn. Children learn not just from the words their teachers speak in the classroom but also from the ways their teachers relate to them, to other teachers, and to the teachers' own families outside of class hour.

LEADERSHIP THROUGH CONSENSUS BUILDING

Learning in community is often a democratic process in which every member of the community has an equal vote. However, an even better method for achieving learning in community is consensus building. This teaching structure is based upon the ability of leaders to build an agreement or consensus among the people rather than just settle for a majority vote. The process of leading through consensus building has been used in some African countries for centuries, and so this process comes to African American leaders through a long cultural tradition. The consensus-building style can be a powerful tool in the hands of a godly Sunday School superintendent who is fully dependent on the Lord for guidance and help in his or her task. A consensus-building superintendent will prayerfully seek to persuade teachers to reach a unity of spirit while humbly listening to what each teacher has to say.

Although some people may think that the leadership of the African American Sunday School is authoritarian, that view is based upon a superficial understanding of the leadership structure. In actuality, decisions are being made as leaders dialogue with the people. The appearance of politics is often due to the need to get people together "on the same page." Leaders take people aside and talk with them in order to persuade people to their point of view. Although they are campaigning for their point of view, they are also listening so that they will understand how the people feel. This is where their strength lies. This is also part of a meaningful dialogue, as dialogue implies searching for similarities (Conradie 1996, 152). The leaders may sometimes give the impression of talking instead of doing, but in reality, dialogue is the most essential part of their leadership. Dialogue is what glues the community together, and it is the most important ingredient in the leadership structure. Although leaders necessarily have strong opinions, they can be persuaded to change their views if they realize through dialogue that they have been wrong.

Having a strong leadership structure is very biblical. The New Testament lists several kinds of leadership in the church (see 1 Corinthians 12:28; Ephesians 4:11–12). Christians differ as to which of these titles are "official," but the Bible seems to indicate that there is some fluidity as to the type of leadership, depending on the context. The Bible also appears to imply that leadership titles may vary depending on the context, even though the gifts and scriptural qualifications required for each type of leadership do not change.

For example, consider the contemporary leadership title of Sunday School superintendent. In the days of Jesus' earthly life, children not only went to synagogue school but were taught by their parents as well (Deuteronomy 6:6–9). Church leaders and teachers continue that tradition today in Sunday School and through the various other children's ministries of the church. They also share with Christian parents how to educate their children in spiritual matters. In the New Testament we read of bishops, elders, and deacons as leaders of the church. In Sunday Schools today, the superintendent is the leader of that ministry. Perhaps the superintendent is a type of deacon. If so, Scripture has some very specific qualifications for someone serving in that role (1 Timothy 3:8–13). The superintendent must be called by God and must have spiritual gifts for the job.

The superintendent's style of leadership will be as varied as the people holding that position. As is the case for each believer, spiritual gifts are conferred in clusters upon those in this role. One superintendent may have a great gift of teaching (Ephesians 4:11); another, a gift of administration (1 Corinthians 12:28); and still another, great wisdom (1 Corinthians 12:8). But each superintendent may have a portion of each of these gifts—some may have more of one gift, and others more of another gift. The nature of the gifts will determine to a large extent how that superintendent carries out his or her responsibilities. The important thing for superintendents to remember is that their gifts are from God and are not to be abused.

The Bible often refers to spiritual leadership. Scripture shows us that church leadership differs from the structure and functioning of leadership in the business world. The CEO may want to ride in limos and have his employees look up to him, while Jesus, our Lord and Savior, humbly washed His disciples' feet (see John 13:1–16) and then told them this was the leadership example they were to follow. Jesus' disciples were forever arguing over who was to be the leader among them and who was to have the highest place of honor in the future kingdom of our Lord. When James and John asked Jesus to let them sit next to Him in His kingdom, Jesus replied by offering Himself as an example of godly leadership: "For even the Son of Man did not come to be served, but to serve, and to give his life as a ransom for many" (Mark 10:45). The best example of sacrificial love and leadership is Jesus' death on the cross for us.

The gospel of John gives us a practical object lesson from the earthly ministry of Jesus in the washing of the disciples' feet. Surely there was no more humble task than to wash the dirty, calloused feet of those men who walked many miles in open sandals on the dusty roads of Palestine. Jesus told His followers,

> Now that I, your Lord and Teacher, have washed your feet, you also should wash one another's feet. I have set you an example that you should do as I have done for you. I tell you the truth, no servant is greater than his master, nor is a messenger greater than the one who sent him. Now that you know these things, you will be blessed if you do them (John 13:14–17).

A Christian leader is to be called of God, spiritually gifted, and a servant-leader.

A Sunday School superintendent has many unglamorous tasks to perform—ordering curriculum, delivering that curriculum on time to the teachers so they can prepare their lessons, seeing that every class has a teacher on Sunday morning, and so on. Just as Jesus' primary task was preparing His disciples for servant-leadership, so the superintendent's primary task is to equip teachers to teach.

Sunday School teachers also demonstrate leadership by teaching students to follow Christ. Just as superintendents must be servant-leaders who are called of God and gifted by the Holy Spirit, so must Sunday School teachers. Sunday School teachers need strong gifts of teaching. Of course, many of us felt intimidated by the task when we first became teachers. When Paul advised young Timothy to "stir up the gift of God, which is in thee" (from 2 Timothy 1:6, KJV), he could also have been speaking to us as teachers. We do not become effective teachers without any effort on our part. There are many different structures for training teachers for Sunday School and other church-education programs, and part of that training includes a time of observation and a time of apprenticeship so that we will be well equipped to teach and address the unique needs of our students. Then, in the beginning years of our teaching ministry, we will be trying out a number of approaches until we find those that suit our own styles. We also need to remember that the same spiritual qualifications that describe the role of superintendent should be ours as well. As we teach children, we should pattern our leadership styles after our Lord Jesus, who washed the disciples' feet. As we follow His example, we will find ourselves helping children, being their advocates, and loving them in a variety of humble ways. Instead of leading through dictatorial methods, we will build a consensus that following Jesus in the best way.

A TRANSMISSIVE APPROACH TO LEARNING

Transmission of content is an important component of a good Bible lesson. It shows that the teacher values what the Word of God says. The apostle Paul spoke to Timothy to remind him of the importance of this method: "What you heard from me, keep as the pattern of sound teaching" (from 2 Timothy 1:13). The psalmist also emphasized the importance of learning all the Bible says when he wrote, "With my lips I recount all the laws that come from your mouth" (Psalm 119:13). We are reminded as well of the supreme importance of God's Word when we realize that Jesus identified Himself as "the Word" (from John 1:1).

The Bible is God's revelation to us and because it is the Word of God, it does not contain only mere facts. Rather, it is a living, dynamic communication from God to us. We read in the New Testament that "the word of God is living and active. Sharper than any double-edged sword, it penetrates even to dividing soul and spirit, joints and marrow; it judges the thoughts and attitudes of the heart" (Hebrews 4:12).

The Bible itself does not purport to be simply a history and fact book, or even just a theological textbook. Spiritual development is not limited to scriptural cognition. It must happen in the affective (emotions and attitude) and volitional (action) realms also. Jesus said that the greatest commandment is to "love the Lord your God with all your heart and with all your soul and with all your mind" (Matthew 22:37). Perhaps this verse covers all three areas of spiritual development, but it is certainly emphasizing the attitude of the heart. We also read in the Bible that God is concerned with what we do (James 1:22) and how we treat one another (James 1:27). These two statements deal with how we act—the volitional realm. In both the volitional area of spiritual growth and the affective realm, methods other than straight lecturing are called for to achieve learning. Memorizing biblical facts alone will not teach anyone to love God. In the volitional realm, the best teaching involves doing. Teachers need to involve children in doing the things that please God. If we are teaching about prayer, children need to be praying, not just be told to pray. If we are teaching children to witness, we need to give them the tools to do so, such as simple words they can use to explain the way of salvation, tracts they can create to tell others about Jesus, and so forth. Even role-playing is a more effective method of teaching children to help others than just telling them to be kind.

In the affective realm, the arts are more effective in touching the hearts and attitudes of our students. A picture of Jesus holding the little children can stir up in the heart of a child a love for our Savior. A song that speaks of the love of Jesus can help children love and worship Him. If we use words to teach children in the affective realm, we will need to use forms that reach the emotions, such as poetry. A heartfelt prayer is also a significant way of touching the attitudes and emotions of children.

The strength of the transmissive approach to learning is in its emphasis on teaching the content of the Bible. The teachers in my study saw Jesus Christ and His Word as the solutions to the problems of the individuals in their community as well as community-wide problems. "What is the rule of the road?" Miss Brooks asked her students. Everyone answered enthusiastically, "Bring your Bible!" The transmission approach is necessary for teaching the substance of the Bible. However, even more important than cognitive content is the importance of a personal relationship with Jesus Christ, as almost all of the teachers emphasized.

Unfortunately, there are some important deficiencies in the transmissive approach to learning. Not only does this method ignore the value of a variety of teaching methods; it also ignores the need for teachers to learn how to communicate biblical truth in ways that children can understand. A dialogical method, on the other hand, is capable of transcending the transmissive method, but only when teachers ask questions that go beyond basic knowledge and help students develop critical thinking.

Another deficiency of the transmissive approach to learning is that it is not well suited to teaching children about relational matters. The emphasis on cognitive content tends to overshadow the equally important emphasis on relationships. Consequently, other teaching styles may be better suited to developing the whole child in the cognitive, affective, and volitional realms.

Although the African American Sunday School teachers in this study primarily used the transmissive mode of instruction, the liveliness of their presentations, their obvious devotion to Jesus, and their love for their students often transcended this one-dimensional mode of teaching to reach the hearts of the children and to inspire them to obey God.

A DIALOGICAL STYLE OF TEACHING

A dialogical approach to teaching is reflective of Black preaching and of God's style of communication with us. In the Garden of Eden, when Adam and Eve were still in a state of innocence, God spoke with the first couple in the cool of the day, as was His custom. After Adam and Eve ate of the fruit of the tree of the knowledge of good and evil, their intimate fellowship and dialogue with God was broken (Genesis 3). But through the Cross, God has restored that fellowship and dialogue between Himself and all those who call upon the name of the Lord Jesus.

A dialogical teaching style makes extensive use of questions. The most commonly used question I noted in my observation of primary classes was, "What did I say?" This reinforces what the teacher just said, and it ensures that students will pay attention. Limited use of this question is useful, but there are better types of questions to ask. The only thing teachers can learn from the answers to this question is that their students can repeat what has been taught. Teachers also need to make sure that students understand what is being said.

Miss Hall, a primary teacher, made frequent use of questions that went beyond mere rote learning to an examination of the children's understanding of biblical knowledge.

When a lesson referred to manna, Miss Hall asked, "Who can tell me what manna is?"

Lawrence quickly raised his hand. "That's when Jesus took a piece of His body and gave it to the people for food," he said as he pantomimed taking a piece of flesh out of his own side.

Such an answer reveals that Lawrence probably heard a previous lesson from John 6, when Jesus said that He is the bread of life, the manna that came down from heaven, but he obviously did not understand the meaning.

Primaries understand things in a very literal manner, so they are especially confused when they hear the parables or similar figurative teachings from the Bible. When Miss Hall asked the children to tell her what manna was, she was checking their understanding. Children can often repeat things they do not understand, but as teachers ask their students to define things or put things into their own words, teachers will not only see how children understand the teaching of the lesson, but they will also teach children to think at a more advanced level.

African American children need to learn critical thinking skills. Learning to define concepts and put things into their own words is just the first step in that process. Critical thinking skills are essential for children to progress in school, but even more important, to learn to interpret their world and thus to become empowered to change their world. Although primaries and juniors are still quite young, African American teachers are building the intellectual and spiritual foundations their students will need as adults.

Beyond recalling and understanding content, which are the first two levels of thinking (see pages 15–17), is the area of applying knowledge to a new situation. We would expect older primary students and juniors to be able to tell what it means to be kind and to give examples. Younger primaries can give more limited examples of kindness, such as sharing. Applying the Bible to children's lives is an important part of Christian education. However, we need to do more than *tell* children how to apply the Bible to their lives; we need to give them the thinking skills to *figure out for themselves* how the Bible might be applied in their own situations. If we tell students to love one another, but they do not understand that beating up someone who just looked at them cross-eyed is not love, then we have failed as teachers. Good questions, such as "How can we honor our parents?" can help students learn to think through and apply biblical principles. Teachers can also tell their students stories about children their own age and ask them what the children in the stories should do. Beyond simple questions, students can be asked to apply biblical principles through role-playing.

Analysis, which is mentally taking ideas apart, is the next level of thinking. Most intelligence tests deal with this level of thinking. Students can demonstrate their analytical abilities by outlining a portion of Scripture. A teacher might first outline the Scripture passage at home to identify the number of logical divisions. Then as the teacher approaches the actual teaching situation, she or he may divide the class into the corresponding number of groups, assign each group one of the Scripture divisions, and instruct each group to make up a title for their section. Then the teacher will write those titles on the chalkboard in the correct order. This is the beginning stage of learning to outline a Scripture passage. Juniors should have no trouble with this type of task.

Seeing the whole picture and drawing conclusions is a higher level of thinking—the level of creative thinking, or synthesis. At this level students can see the broad general principles of the Bible. One type of question to ask students at this level is to summarize the lesson. Juniors should be able to do this, and even primaries may be challenged in this area, although primaries may wander away from the plot or main message of the lesson. Juniors should be doing more advanced thinking than this.

The highest level of learning through questions is evaluation. This is beyond the thinking level of primaries and juniors.

The dialogical style of African American teachers is lively and keeps the attention of students. It can also be a wonderful means of guiding students into higher-order thinking in which questions go beyond merely asking children to parrot the words.

A FIRM BELIEF THAT
JESUS CHRIST IS THE ANSWER

The most wonderful strength of the African American church is the belief of her members in the Lord Jesus Christ and His Word. Some have criticized the

African American church for holding back on current trends in Christian education, but this has kept the Sunday School program on track, spiritually speaking.
Talking vegetables and gimmicky toys may be fun, but African Americans hunger
for the meat of the Word. Among other groups of American Christians, Sunday
School attendance may be faltering, but African American children are still going to Sunday School. Even African American adults are committed to biblical
education in the church.

The basic truths of the Word were obviously dear to the African American Sunday School teachers I observed, but they also found some other biblical passages
especially relevant. When the narratives regarding the slavery of the Hebrews in
Egypt were discussed, teachers always expanded upon the African American experiences of slavery. Mr. Jones said, "Those times were hard, but God helped the
slaves. Sunday School teachers are supposed to remind children of what God has
done for them and for their people."

Teachers often asked the children to relate those times to current problems.
Sometimes the children were called upon to recall the oral traditions of the elders
in their own families. But the teachers did not just apply the story of God's de-
livery of His people from slavery in Egypt to the situation of African Americans
who were once enslaved in this country. Ms. Green said, "Not accepting Christ as
Savior from sin is the same thing as being in slavery." And Mr. Brown said, "Just
as we need to remember the days of African American enslavement, so we need
to recall the time of our salvation."

Paulo Freire speaks of a community's right to interpret its own history and choose
its own heroes. Miss Wilson spoke of the children's love of the conquering aspects
of the Bible, and she said that the theme she chose for her students this year is
"Developing a Conquering Mind-Set." This is truly not a concept that young primaries can understand, but it speaks to the right of African American Christians to
interpret the Bible for their own community. Taken to an extreme, this would mean
that each people group would retain the right to its own interpretation of the Holy
Scriptures, but a more orthodox view is that the Bible can be interpreted contextu-
ally without denying the absolute nature of the truth contained in God's Word.

All of the African American Sunday School teachers I observed in this study were
actively interpreting their world through the lens of Scripture. Some teachers saw

the sufficiency of Christ for whatever problems we face in life; others saw in the Bible a theology of striving. Those in the latter group sought to teach traits that would help the children succeed in the mainstream culture. Some may scorn African American religious education for inculcating in learners middle-class socio-economic ethics, but it is important to keep in mind that some of the methods effectively equip members of the African American community with skills to survive the challenges of life.

Conclusion

In this chapter we have examined five characteristics of African American teaching styles to find the strengths in each and to see how we can build upon them. Since these are the styles of teaching and learning in the African American community, all teachers of African American children, regardless of their own color or ethnicity, will increase the effectiveness of their teaching by incorporating these styles that are most familiar to the children.

Reference List

Conradie, Ernst. Tracy's notion of dialogue: "Our last, best hope?" *Scriptura 57* (1996):149–178.

Roberts, J. Deotis. *Black Theology in Dialogue.* Philadelphia: The Westminster Press, 1987.

PART III: NOW LET'S TEACH!

CHAPTER 7

USING TEACHING OBJECTIVES

Teaching without objectives is like hopping on a train without knowing where you are going. How will you know when you arrive if you do not know your destination? Written objectives not only help us keep in mind what we want to accomplish in our teaching, but they also help us evaluate whether our children are growing in the Lord. Without objectives, we may think that we are just going to "teach the lesson." This will probably lead us to make sure our students learn the biblical content, but just learning "the facts" is not a true Christian education. God desires that beyond mere head knowledge, our hearts would be changed and our lives and actions would be affected by what we learn. The twin goals of written objectives are (1) to define what we want to happen in the lives of our students, and (2) to work toward making those things happen by the way we teach.

THREE KINDS OF TEACHING OBJECTIVES

As in the chapter on spiritual development, we must remember that spiritual growth needs to take place in three areas or realms: knowledge, attitude, and action. Objectives can speak to these areas of spiritual growth, and we must not neglect any of these areas when we plan our lessons.

Formulating Knowledge Objectives

Objectives in the cognitive or knowledge area will focus on learning what the Bible says. The goal of the cognitive objective is for children to grow spiritually in the area of biblical knowledge. This goes beyond learning to answer questions about what we as teachers say. We want our students to *understand* what we, and the Bible, are saying. Knowing how to apply the teachings of the Scriptures is the third level of cognition. We want to make sure children are able to know what God wants them to do.

A knowledge objective will sound something like this:

- Level 1: That the students will know that God created our earth.
- Level 2: That the students will understand that God created them in His image.
- Level 3: That the students will know how to apply love in their relationships with others.
- Level 4: That the students will analyze the Bible story and tell it in sequential order.
- Level 5: That the students will be able to summarize the message in the book of Jonah (or maybe summarize the whole Bible!).
- Level 6: That the students will evaluate their lives in the light of the teaching of God's Word.

Determining what level of knowledge is appropriate for students depends on their stage of development. For primaries the objectives will be, for the most part, on the first three cognitive levels (knowledge, understanding, and application). Juniors should be able to accomplish objectives on the fourth and fifth levels as well (analysis and synthesis).

Formulating Attitude Objectives

Objectives in the affective realm will focus on the expression of attitudes and feelings. God is very concerned with what is going on in the hearts of our students. The attitude or affective objective is aimed right at the heart. Here are a few examples of attitude objectives:

1. That the students will be sorry for their sins.
2. That the students will express love toward the Lord.
3. That the students will be thankful for the gifts God gives them.

Formulating Action Objectives

Objectives in the volitional or action realm are phrased differently to achieve a different purpose. In this area we want to see our students actively obeying the Lord, and so we will see a variety of action verbs in the objectives. Here are a few examples:

1. That the students will share with one another.
2. That the students will bring canned goods for the church food pantry.
3. That the students will pray before they go to bed.

The action verbs in each of these objectives (share, bring, pray) state something we want the students to do.

FORMULATING OBJECTIVES TO ACCOMPLISH HOLISTIC SPIRITUAL GROWTH

A good lesson always has three objectives—one for each area of spiritual development—and all three of these objectives should be related to one another. For instance, a lesson on the story of Nicodemus coming to Jesus by night and learning how to be born again (John 3:1–18) will have a threefold objective:

- *Knowledge:* That the students will learn the plan of salvation.
- *Attitude:* That the students will be thankful that Jesus died on the cross to save them.
- *Action:* That the students will ask the Lord to save them.

Every part of the lesson should be geared toward accomplishing the objectives.

In the lesson on John 3:1–18, we might have the children memorize an outline on the way of salvation and perhaps a Bible verse to go with each point. We want to be sure that the children understand this very important lesson. This would help achieve the knowledge or cognitive objective. For the action objective, we would want to see children receive Christ as Savior. In this lesson, we want to be especially sure to pray that those who say they want to be saved (born again) are truly being led by the Holy Spirit. This makes the action objective also part of the attitude objective. Are children really thankful that God loves them and sent His Son to take their punishment for sin? Are they truly convicted of their need for a Savior?

Planning Based upon Objectives

A week before teaching my lesson, I look at the printed curriculum to see both the stated objectives and the Scripture passage. As I read through the passage, I pray that God will fulfill these objectives in my students' lives. I pray this every day. Sometimes I see that the stated objectives would not be best for my students, so I read through the passage again to see what the Bible is saying that God can use in their lives. Are the objectives achievable for my students with God's help? Sometimes the most obvious lesson of a passage is more appropriate for the understanding level of adults, so I try to ascertain what objectives I can draw for the children in my class.

After determining that the stated objectives are good ones for my students, I read through the lesson to see how each part supports achieving the objectives. A good lesson will use every activity listed in the plan to reach the stated objectives. As I prepare I ask myself a number of questions: Are the songs and prayers in line with the objectives? Are there activities other than those in the lesson plan that would better accomplish the objectives? How does the telling and teaching of the Bible lesson itself lead students to achieve the objectives? How can I make the routines of my class come in line with the objectives? For instance, how can I make the offering an activity that reinforces the objectives?

Most adults come away from a lesson or sermon with two or three thoughts, but lessons for children should focus on just one thought and its threefold objectives.

DID THE TRAIN ARRIVE AT THE STATION?

If we have taught with well-defined objectives, we can evaluate whether those objectives have been accomplished in the lives of our students. We will know whether our students have arrived at the station—if they have grasped the knowledge we have attempted to convey.

Perhaps on Sunday afternoon, when you have finished your dinner, you can sit in your favorite chair and open your Bible and your teacher's lesson plan. Or take a quick look at the objectives immediately after a Vacation Bible School class or a weekly children's club. As you review the objectives, think back reflectively as to whether they have been met.

To evaluate whether knowledge (cognitive) objectives have been met, we can reflect on the questions we asked our students and the answers they gave, whether written or spoken. Our questions should probe the understanding of the learners, such as "What does _____ mean?" "Define _____ (what is such and such?)," and "Put that in your own words."

Attitude (affective) objectives are the hardest to measure. We turn to the Bible and see that only "God knows [our] hearts" (from Luke 16:15), and yet we also see that the attitude of the heart is very important to Him (1 Samuel 16:7). Jesus said that the two most important commandments are that we should love the Lord our God with all our heart, soul, mind, and strength and that we should love our neighbor as ourselves (Mark 12:30–31). With this in mind, we plan the attitude objectives and pray that the Holy Spirit would accomplish them in the hearts of our students, just as we pray that all of the objectives might be accomplished.

Evaluating the action (volitional) objectives is the easiest thing to do from an educational standpoint. Action objectives are what educators call behavioral objectives. Behavioral objectives are measurable, realistic, and achievable. Are the children sharing with one another? Are they telling others about Christ? Are they being kind to children who are different from them? These are all actions we can look at and evaluate. When the Bible says, "By their fruit you will recognize them" (from Matthew 7:16), it means that we are authorized to measure the works of other Christians. Teachers are ordained to do that in their students' lives. So go ahead. Look at the things your students are doing to see if the action objectives are being accomplished.

CHAPTER 8

LEADING CHILDREN TO CHRIST

Can children be saved? Can they be born again? Jesus said, "Let the little children come to me, and do not hinder them, for the kingdom of heaven belongs to such as these" (Matthew 19:14). Jesus also used a child as an example of the type of faith needed to enter the kingdom of heaven: "I tell you the truth, unless you change and become like little children, you will never enter the kingdom of heaven" (Matthew 18:3). Therefore, we can see that children are not only capable of trusting Jesus as Savior, but their faith is the kind God is looking for.

To be saved is the most important thing in the life of a boy, girl, man, or woman. We look at the followers of Jesus in the New Testament and see many examples of individuals who were converted in a wonderful way as they realized their own sinful inadequacy and threw themselves at Jesus' feet and placed their trust in His blood, which He shed on the cross for us. Just think about the stories of the apostle Paul, Cornelius, the Philippian jailer, the Ethiopian official, and Lydia.

In the Bible the terms *born again* (John 3:3) and saved (Acts 16:31) are synonymous, and God says we all need this experience of regeneration when we cast ourselves on the Lord Jesus and trust in His sacrifice for our sins to make us right with God. What does it mean to be "saved" or "born again"? God has a definite plan of salvation, and this plan begins with conversion. Conversion is the doorway to salvation. It is a once-for-all, never-to-be-repeated event. It is an action, not a feeling.

Two things are required of us for salvation: *repentance* and *faith*. We need to be truly sorry for our sins and make a complete turn to God. True repentance can only come about when we are convicted of our sinfulness by the Holy Spirit. Repentance means a sincere change of mind and heart toward God.

Faith involves trusting in what the Lord Jesus did for us on the cross. It means believing in God's Word and trusting in Christ. Believing is the opposite of doing something to save ourselves. It is trusting only in the Lord. We are helpless to save ourselves; only God is able to save us. Salvation is the work of God by which He rescues us from the punishment for our sin and gives us eternal life both now and in the life to come.

Regeneration and *justification* are terms that denote God's part in our salvation. *Justification* is the judicial act of God whereby He declares us righteous before Him. He does this on the grounds of Christ's atoning work on the cross, by grace through faith alone, apart from works.

Regeneration is the theological term for being born again. It is the work of the Holy Spirit in giving a new nature, a new life, and a new heart to the believer. Only this new birth makes fellowship with God possible.

The moment we believe and are saved, we receive many free gifts—full pardon from sin, acceptance in God's sight, adoption as His children, eternal life, the gift of the Holy Spirit, and the power to live lives pleasing to God.

THE AGE OF UNDERSTANDING SALVATION

The next question is, "When are children old enough to be saved?" We believe that our just and loving Heavenly Father would not condemn children to hell before they know right from wrong, but when children are old enough to make these decisions they are accountable to God with regard to the salvation decision. Theologians have called this the *age of accountability*. God's Word does not give us any clues regarding when children are old enough to receive Christ, but social science helps us understand children and the way they think. Since this social science is a study of God's wonderful creation—the minds of those He created—we can see if what it says helps us understand salvation in the context of the cognitive and moral development of children.

Piaget viewed the formation of morals as dependent upon cognitive development. I believe we can also say that spiritual development is dependent upon moral and cognitive development. Piaget observed that children act primarily on impulse from ages 2 through 7. After this they are capable of using reason in acts of their will. Then children choose what is right to do based upon the logical deduction of what is fair and honest. When children choose what is right over what is pleasurable, they must choose the superior thing to do instead of what is easiest. Based upon the findings of Piaget, we would say that before the age of 6 or 7, children are not capable of making true moral choices. However, sometime during the primary years or surely during the junior years, children reach the wonderful age when they can first truly understand and believe the Good News of salvation.

Salvation is a gift of God that is so complex that we as adults cannot completely understand it, and yet it is so simple that even a child can understand it well enough to be born again (saved). Explaining the way of salvation with a simple outline will surely omit many other ways that people come to Christ. Some who were raised in Christian homes are hardly aware of the moment when they first came to believe. Others find Christ as adults when cataclysmic changes take place in their lives.

During the preschool years, children obey simply to please their parents, teachers, or other significant people in their lives. Because they do not understand the concept of rules, they do not understand that rules must be obeyed, even when their parents are unaware of what they are doing. This is the age of soil fertilization when we teach preschoolers that God loves them and wants them to obey Him. Teaching these concepts is important to prepare children for future decisions for Christ. Then when seeds of the Gospel are sown at a later age, these boys and girls will be ready to receive the Lord Jesus Christ as Savior.

Primaries are beginning to understand the concept of rules, so they can understand that God has rules that must be obeyed. Although primaries do not understand the abstract idea of "sin," they can understand "sins" as individual acts of disobedience. We can begin explaining salvation to children by telling them that sin is doing anything God does not want us to do. We might explain it this way: "Maybe we have taken something that does not belong to us or talked back to our mamas or hurt someone, but all of these things are sins, and all of us have sinned."

The terminology of salvation is often confusing to children. They may hear a variety of expressions referring to the same thing, such as "Ask Jesus to come into your heart," "Ask Jesus to give you a new heart," "Become a Christian," "Ask Jesus to save you," or "Pray to be born again." If you ask children to name some different ways to say "born again," you will help them understand that all of these terms mean the same thing. Saved and born again are good biblical terms meaning the same thing, but the phrases "Ask Jesus into your heart" or "Ask Jesus to give you a new heart" can be confusing to children, especially to literally-minded primaries. Some may think that Jesus must be very little if He can fit into someone's heart. Others may wonder how many Jesuses there are if He is in your heart as well as theirs.

Some Christian teachers use beads or a book with pages of different colors to explain the way of salvation. They say that white represents a sinless heart while black equals sin. This approach not only reinforces a racist mind-set among White children, but it also undermines the self-esteem of Black children. Substituting the word *dark* for *black* just increases the number of people who are offended by color categorization of sin. The Bible uses only one color when referring to sin: red "like scarlet" (Isaiah 1:18).

In addition to their confusion about terminology, primaries may think that they need to be saved or born again each time a teacher or pastor talks about it. They may also think that they need to be "born again" even though they have already been "saved." Or they may think they need to be saved every time they sin. We need to tell the children that they are saved because they have believed in Jesus, and no one or nothing can take that away from them.

Many juniors have not yet accepted Jesus as Savior and are now ready to be saved. Although they will not have as many areas of confusion as do primaries, we still need to be careful how we explain salvation to them. While primaries may respond to a salvation appeal to please their teachers, juniors are apt to come forward in response to an invitation when they see their friends coming. They want to do what their friends are doing. Rather than having students come forward in response to an invitation, it is better to tell them to come talk with you after class or to silently repeat a prayer asking Jesus to save them as you say it aloud phrase by phrase. These two techniques help assure that juniors make professions of faith that are genuine.

A SIMPLE WAY TO EXPLAIN SALVATION

It is so easy to be saved or born again that we can tell children the way using the ABCs. This simple device will help children organize their thinking and will help them remember the most important decision they can make. Here is this simple outline: A—Ask Jesus to forgive your sins. B—Believe that Jesus died on the cross to take the punishment for your sins. C—Call on Jesus to save you (make you born again).

First, we explain what sin is. Sin is doing anything God does not want us to do. Then we need to name specific sins that almost all children have committed, such as hurting someone or taking something that does not belong to them. We tell children that God is so holy and so wonderful that He cannot stand to have anyone around Him who has sinned. That means that none of us can go to heaven to live with God, because all of us have sinned. But God loves us so much that He sent Jesus to die on the cross to take the punishment for our sins. Then we tell children that when they do something wrong, they are punished. Their teacher punishes them when they break his or her rules. Their parents punish them when they do not obey the rules. None of us has obeyed all of God's rules, but God did not want to punish us, and so He sent His Son, Jesus, to be punished instead of us. Jesus was punished for us when He died on the cross. We finish by saying that God wants us to believe that Jesus died for us. When we believe, He promises us that we will be saved and go to heaven when we die.

THE INVITATION FOR SALVATION

We want to make sure that children do not respond to salvation invitations for reasons other than genuine conviction by the Holy Spirit. As I mentioned earlier, if we ask children to come forward to accept Christ, they may do so to please their teacher, to follow their friends, or to receive a reward. One solution is to ask children to come talk with their teacher after class. If they truly want to be saved, they will not mind leaving play with their friends to take care of this most important business. The teacher may then go over the plan of salvation with the child who is seeking salvation. Ask the child what each letter—*A, B, C*—stands for, and what that means. As you and the child discuss the letter *A*—Ask Jesus to forgive your sins—look up the following verse and ask the child to read it: "For all have sinned and fall short of the glory of God" (Romans 3:23). Explain that "[falling] short of the glory of God" means that we are not good and perfect like God is.

As you discuss the letter *B*—Believe that Jesus died on the cross to take the punishment for your sins—look up the following verse: "For God so loved the world that he gave his one and only Son, that whoever believes in him shall not perish but have eternal life" (John 3:16). Talk with the child about how Jesus took our punishment when He died on the cross.

Discuss the letter *C*—Call on Jesus to save you (make you born again). Look up the following verse and ask the student to read it: "Everyone who calls on the name of the Lord will be saved" (Romans 10:13). Ask the student, "What promise does God make in this verse?" Then answer, "Yes, He promises to save everyone who calls on His name." Next ask the student, "How do we call upon the Lord?" and answer, "In prayer." Invite the student to ask the Lord to save him or her. If the student hesitates, you may pray as he or she repeats these words: "Dear Lord, I am sorry for my sins. Please forgive me. Thank You for loving me and sending Jesus to the cross to die for me. Please save me now. Amen."

Sometimes the situation does not allow us to ask children to come talk with us after class. In such situations, I carefully review the plan of salvation with the class. Then I invite those who want to be saved right then to silently pray the prayer I mentioned in the previous paragraph. I say one short phrase at a time and allow time for silent repetition. Then I tell the children that if they prayed that prayer, they should tell someone they think would like to know, such as their teacher, their pastor, or their parents. I think that is in keeping with the Scripture: "If you confess with your mouth, 'Jesus is Lord,' and believe in your heart that God raised him from the dead, you will be saved" (Romans 10:9).

ASSURANCE OF SALVATION

When I was 8 years old, I prayed silently every night before going to bed: "Lord, if I'm not saved yet, save me now." Finally, I realized that I did not have to pray over and over for salvation. Many children come forward each time an altar call is given. Even adults pray for salvation a number of times before they are sure they are really saved. When we counsel children for salvation, we always begin by asking if they have ever done something like this before. When we hear their responses, the Holy Spirit will guide us to know whether they have already been saved before. If the children describe some experience that indicates they did not understand at that time that they were accepting Jesus' offer of salvation, they probably have not been born again, and we can lead them to a genuine spiritual rebirth. If some say that they went to the front of the church or were baptized, we ask them why they did this. If nothing they say indicates that they understand that Jesus died to bring them salvation, then we need to go through the way of salvation again to help them truly accept Christ's death on the cross for them. If they seem to have understood what is involved in being born again in a prior experience, we can help them find an assurance of salvation and let them know that they only need to pray for salvation once. God always answers that prayer. Look at Romans 10:13 again to see God's promise: "Everyone who calls on the name of the Lord will be saved."

Another Step for Juniors

At each stage of development, God calls upon us to make a renewed and deeper commitment to Jesus. Many juniors are ready to take another step, especially if their original time of salvation was when they were still primaries. For primaries, salvation is a gift from God, and they can be challenged to obey Christ through individual acts. Juniors can make a bigger commitment to whole-life obedience. I like to tell the story of Shadrach, Meshach, and Abednego, who bravely obeyed the Lord without any regard for the consequences. When Nebuchadnezzar threatened to throw them into a fiery furnace if they would not bow down to his idol, they answered,

> If we are thrown into the blazing furnace, the God we serve is able to save us from it, and he will rescue us from your hand, O king. But even if he does not, we want you to know, O king, that we will not serve your gods or worship the image of gold you have set up (Daniel 3:17–18).

Prayerfully challenge juniors to promise to obey God even when it is hard to do.

CHAPTER 9

LEARNING IN COOPERATION WITH ONE ANOTHER

Consider this passage from the Old Testament:

> Two are better than one,
> because they have a good return for their work:
> If one falls down,
> his friend can help him up.
> But pity the man who falls
> and has no one to help him up!…
> Though one may be overpowered,
> two can defend themselves.
> A cord of three strands is not quickly broken
> (Ecclesiastes 4:9–10, 12).

God created us for community. Even God Himself is a community of three-in-one. When God said, "Let us make man in our image, in our likeness" (from Genesis 1:26), He made us to mirror the fellowship of the Trinity. God said, "It is not good for . . . man to be alone" (from Genesis 2:18), and so He created a human complement and partner for Adam: Eve. Men and women were created to live in fellowship, love, and community.

After Adam and Eve sinned, conflict entered into that community. "She made me do it," said Adam. "The snake made me do it," said Eve (Genesis 3:12–13, author's paraphrase). Because of pride, humankind competed with one another, and wars and fighting arose. Human nature is designed by God for community, but sin interferes and conflicts result. A strong Christian-education methodology considers God's original design for community and works toward that, but it is also cognizant of the human tendency toward sinfulness. God desires us to work together in cooperation and community, but such skills and attitudes need to be taught.

When Jesus came, He gave us a new community—the church. The church is meant to reflect the unity of the Father with the Son (John 17:20–21). The church is a fellowship like a family or a team. The fellowship found within the Black church has been a great source of strength and comfort to the African American community throughout its history.

Christian community demands educational methods that are in accord with God's design for the church. The methods that are best suited to bringing about what God wants us to be are those that foster cooperation, love, and community.

Unfortunately, the methodology of Christian education has often been based on the sociological context of its time. The United States of America has a history of hardy individualism, and so competitive teaching methods have been very popular in Christian education as well as secular education. However, just as Socrates and Aristotle built their methodology on their philosophy, Christian-education methods should be based upon biblically-based philosophy or theology. A doctrine of humankind created by God as a community should lead to an educational method that bases its style of teaching and learning on cooperation.

Competition is not the way to achieve community. Although Scripture uses analogies such as the runner competing for the prize, the picture is of believers meeting God's standards rather than competing against one another. Competition in today's world is usually based on one person winning while everyone else loses. The winner gets the prize only at the expense of others. Competition, as viewed in Scripture, is more like the criterion-referenced achievement spoken of by modern educators. If all reach the criteria, all may win. Thus, the participant is competing against the standard rather than the other participants. Viewed from this perspective, competition is not unbiblical and is a good method for introducing variety into teaching methods. Even so, cooperative learning is the method of education that is most in tune with biblical theology.

THE DEFINITION OF COOPERATIVE LEARNING

Cooperative or collaborative learning is a process whereby students work together as a team to accomplish shared goals. Good cooperative learning includes the following three characteristics: team rewards, individual accountability, and equal opportunities for success. Merely seating children next to each other physically is not enough for true cooperative learning. Assigning a project to the group is not enough either. Team members need to depend upon one another for true cooperative learning to take place. Then when the goal is accomplished, the entire team may be rewarded with small prizes, certificates, or words of praise. Using individual competition rewards just a few children. The others resent them and their success, and they may call them "nerds." Beyond 7 years of age, children are more interested in pleasing their peers than their teachers, which makes cooperative learning superior for students at this level.

Cooperative learning must avoid the trap of allowing some team members to do all the work while others are just along for the ride. This will inevitably lead to feelings of resentment. Designing teamwork to include individual accountability will overcome this disadvantage.

While cooperative methods are appropriate for all types of learning situations, they are especially good for conceptual tasks. The more problem solving, decision making, and creativity required in a task, the more appropriate the choice of cooperative instructional methods. Collaborative or cooperative learning is also good for long-term memory, higher-level thinking, and social development of students.

THE ADVANTAGES OF COOPERATIVE LEARNING

Educators have noticed that although all children do well with cooperative learning methods, Black children do especially well in such an environment (Allen and Boykin 1992). Maybe this is due to African cultural traditions or the need for African Americans to pull together when shut out by the mainstream culture. Or maybe it is because of the special influence of the fellowship bonds created in

African American churches all across America. Whatever the reason, learning in community, or cooperative learning, matches both the style of the African American church community and the teaching of the Bible. Let's consider some of the advantages of cooperative learning.

First, cooperative learning helps children develop greater thinking abilities. When we listen to others share their perspectives, even our own views change. Our thinking is enriched because we are looking at things from a variety of angles. Sunday School classes and children's church clubs comprise different individuals. Some are bouncy and outgoing; others are quiet and reflective. Some children enjoy reading; others prefer physical activities. Some come from large families; others are the only child in their homes. These and many other variables make the collaborative learning environment a place where every child can benefit from the strengths of others, and every child has something to contribute. This kind of learning also leads children to mature in their own thinking processes.

Although cooperation or collaboration is a good method for all types of learning, it is especially good for teaching concepts. As students listen to one another and explain their own reasoning to the group, their thinking is challenged. Learning to look at ideas from different perspectives helps students perform higher-order thinking, develops their language skills, and encourages creativity.

In addition to developing cognitive skills, cooperation contributes to the development of positive self-esteem by building students' confidence in their relational skills. Working in groups with members having various abilities, gifts, and experiences increases the students' respect for one another. In addition, even the students with the lowest levels of cognitive ability have a chance to win with their team if abilities are equally distributed in the group. Thus, cooperative learning increases more than just understanding of concepts; it also teaches children how to work together and enjoy it.

Third, cooperative methodology is active learning. Children are much more likely to remember things they have experienced and discovered for themselves. Learning to work together and play together is an important part of what we want to teach our students.

PUTTING COOPERATIVE LEARNING INTO PRACTICE

Interpersonal and small-group skills must be taught. We cannot assume that students will automatically know how to function well in a group. Collaboration is a conglomeration of learned skills, and cooperative instruction uses intentional methods to teach these skills. The following sections give some ideas on how to implement cooperative learning in the classroom.

Dividing the Class into Teams

In some approaches to cooperative learning, the children are divided into teams. The best teams are composed of a diversity of students. In other words, children on the team will be on different learning levels and will come from a variety of home backgrounds. One method of dividing students into teams is to use name tags of different colors with each color representing a different team. But do not let the children know about this code until you are ready to divide them into groups. Another way is to have students number off and gather into groups with corresponding numbers. A third method is to cut up pictures into four or fives pieces each (jigsaw-puzzle style) and give each child part of a picture. Then have the children search for other students who have the pieces to complete their pictures. Those with one complete picture comprise one team, and so forth.

A VARIETY OF APPROACHES TO COOPERATIVE LEARNING

In another approach to cooperative learning, the children teach each other. First, the teacher presents the lesson. Then the children work in pairs or small groups to help one another learn the material. You may quiz the children individually on the materials and add up the individual points for the team. This motivates the children to help one another so that their team will do well. As the children work together and help the members of their team, they are learning the skills needed for learning in community.

Another way to incorporate cooperative learning in the classroom is through team investigation. The teacher chooses a broad topic, and each team works together to choose a subtopic. Then the teacher circulates among the groups and oversees them. This method can easily be used in the Sunday School context. The teacher may assign the topic "The History of Our Church," and each team may choose a particular era in the history of their neighborhood church to research. They may use such resources as interviews and newspaper clippings for their research and then present the material to the rest of the class in a creative way, such as presenting a mural with narration. Another topic might be "Life in Galilee in Jesus' Day" with individual teams researching the food in Jesus' day, the type of homes, fishing, and so forth. The teams may present their information in a variety of ways, including skits, newspapers, scrapbooks, musicals, raps, or dances.

Games in the Cooperative Learning Style

Games are a large component of cooperative instruction, and they work well because they are fun.

"Numbered Heads Together" is simple, fun, and incorporates the characteristics of effective team learning. The members of each team are numbered, beginning with the number one in each team. The teacher begins the game by posing a question. The groups assemble and discuss the answer, making sure that each team member has the correct answer. After several minutes, the teacher flicks off the light, indicating that discussion time is over and everyone must be quiet. Then the teacher calls out a number, and as the light goes back on, each student who has that number in each group raises his or her hand. The student who is able to answer the question correctly for his or her team receives points for the team.

"Team Game Tournaments" begin with three representatives from three different teams sitting at each table. The three individuals at each table are then given a written quiz. The representative doing the best job on the quiz receives points for his or her team.

Another game is "Memory-Verse Pairs." The children are divided into pairs to teach each other the Bible memory verse. Then the teacher pulls the name of a student from a hat or a jar. If that child can recite the verse correctly, the child and his or her partner receive small prizes, such as stickers. The teacher may quiz as many pairs as time allows and interest continues. The strong point of this activity is that peer tutoring reinforces both the learning of the tutor and the student being tutored. Most children also learn better from a peer tutor.

Play the game "Reading Teams" by dividing the children into pairs to read the Bible lesson to each other. They summarize the passage to each other, write different endings to the story, engage in assigned vocabulary activities, or engage in other interesting activities. After the team activities, all individuals answer written quizzes and prizes are awarded to the teams who answer the questions correctly.

"Round Robin" begins with four or five students sitting around a table to discuss a question, problem, or concept that the teacher has given them. Going around the table clockwise or counterclockwise, each student contributes an idea about the topic being discussed.

"Round Table" is similar to "Round Robin," but the students brainstorm on paper. Each child has a different color marker or pen, and a piece of paper is passed around so that each student can add his or her ideas. Continue passing the paper around the table for additional ideas. When a student cannot think of an idea, he or she may ask another student for help or "pass" on his or her turn. A group reporter from each team will share the team responses.

"Interview" is another enjoyable collaborative activity. Two students interview each other on the same topic. First, one of the students asks questions and listens, then the roles are reversed. Two pairs may even join together for a four-member round robin in which each student shares the responses of the person he or she interviewed.

TEACHING COOPERATIVE LEARNING SKILLS

Cooperative learning skills are necessary for our growth as the body of Christ as well as for functioning in today's society in which social interaction is necessary in almost every area of life. However, social skills do not come naturally; they must be taught. Research is showing that the earlier a child is taught cooperative learning skills, the better. Even preschoolers can learn to work together.

The first step in developing cooperative learning skills is creating the right atmosphere. Even the way a room is arranged affects how children interact. Arrange the chairs so the children are facing one another, or facing their team members if they have been divided into teams. Even a specific area of the classroom can be devoted to team activities. Decorate the classroom or designated area with poster boards containing teamwork slogans and rules, such as the following:

1. Let everyone have a turn to talk.
2. Tell someone in your group, "Good idea!" or "That's a good thought."
3. A good team works together.
4. Be a good listener, even when you do not agree.
5. Try to understand what others are saying.
6. If you do not understand, tell people what you think they are saying.
7. Criticize ideas, not people.

You may promise individual and team rewards for keeping the group rules. Finally, choosing team names can help develop team spirit.

The second step in developing cooperative learning skills is teaching the actual skills. This involves demonstrating the skill, defining it, describing it, and then demonstrating it again. Ask students to role-play the skills. List phrases that may be used in their presentation, such as "Do you agree?" and "How would you explain the answer?" Some of the skills to be taught are these: (1) restating the purpose of the assignment; (2) expressing support for others' contributions; (3) asking for clarification; (4) offering to clarify ideas; (5) paraphrasing what has been said; (6) energizing the group when needed with new ideas, enthusiasm, and humor; and (7) describing feelings when appropriate. Primaries may learn skills such as adding an idea, asking for proof, and seeing ideas from others' viewpoints. Teach just one or two skills at a time.

Using the skills is the third step in developing cooperative learning. Set up practice situations so that collaborative skills can be used often enough to become part of the students' regular behavior. Integrate skills into automatic behavior patterns. Encourage children to persevere until they have learned the skills. Assign roles to each person in a group, such as facilitator, observer, recorder, summarizer, and encourager. Tell the students that you will be observing them, and use a checklist to tally the number of times specific skills are used. Also teach the students how to use the observation checklist.

Evaluation As a Component of Cooperative Learning

Allow 10 minutes at the end of each Sunday School class period for a time to evaluate the cooperation skills used by the groups that day. During this time ask the students to identify problems and compare their performances with the desired standard. Feedback should be positive as well as immediate, specific, and descriptive. Ask each participant to describe a specific thing a team member did to use cooperative skills effectively. Give the students a checklist for the desired collaborative skills. After the team decides which skills they accomplished that day and check them off, all the individual members should sign the list.

Conclusions

Although competitive and individualistic methods may be included in lessons to introduce variety, cooperative methods are the most biblical for Christian education. Properly used, cooperative methods will create a model of the church within the Sunday School classroom. The students will share their gifts, abilities, and varying perspectives to build one another up in the Lord. And they will function together as a community of love, faith, and unity. The only caveat is that it is not enough for churches to have teachers who are skilled at using collaborative methods but are not working for Christ and His kingdom. It is far better to have teachers who love the Lord, His Word, and their students.

Reference List

Boykin, Wade and Brenda Allen. "African American children and the educational process: Alleviating cultural discontinuity through prescriptive pedagogy." *School Psychology Review*, 21 (1992): 586–596.

Johnson, David W. and Roger T. Johnson. *Learning Together and Alone: Cooperative, Competitive, and Individualistic Learning.* Boston: Allyn and Bacon, 1994.

CHAPTER 10

READING THE WORD

Sister Smith was recognized as an excellent primary Sunday School teacher. Not only did she have the spiritual gift of teaching and spent a great deal of time preparing her lessons, but she was also a public school teacher. Her years of studying to be an elementary school teacher taught her much about how children learn. One skill was especially important in teaching Sunday School: the ability to teach children how to read. Reading in Sunday School is very important. God gave us His Word to read, and so we need to master this skill. Reading the written Sunday School materials is a stepping-stone to reading the Bible, but teaching our students to read takes much more than simply thrusting the lessons in front of them, especially for primaries.

When first graders enter Sister Smith's primary class in September, they are just beginning to learn to read. Most cannot read much more than their own names. So before Sister Smith puts the written lesson in front of the children, she tells the Bible story. During the week, she has studied her lesson and knows the Bible story so well that she does not need to read it from her teachers' guide. She even practices telling the Bible story to her son. When it is time to tell the story to her class, she tells it dramatically and with passion.

Then she is ready to distribute the written Sunday School material. When her students take their turns to read aloud, she listens carefully to see how well they can read. She may ask the first graders to read the first sentence together. Then she asks them to repeat it several times. This will help them learn to read the words. Then it is time for more advanced readers to take their turns. She knows that silent reading is an important skill to learn, so she tells the children to read to themselves before they read aloud, and she asks them one or two questions to think about while they are reading. Then when the students have finished reading the material, she asks the questions again to see who is reading for meaning.

Next it is time to read the material aloud. Sister Smith considers her students' abilities when she asks them to read orally. If children are missing more than one word per sentence, the reading material is probably too hard for them. When we think about reading levels, we must remember that they only represent averages. For instance, half of the second graders in a class will read above level, and half will read below level. A good teacher assigns work that is neither too easy nor too hard so that students will be challenged rather than discouraged. Sister Smith uses the *whole-language approach* when she teaches her second graders in public school. This approach suggests that there is more to literacy than just recognizing written words. A good reading program encompasses all of language—reading, writing, and even oral language skills, such as listening. Listening is one aspect of the whole-language approach. Students may listen to stories on audiotapes or videos, or to stories the teacher reads or tells them. Students tell stories by acting or writing them out; drawing pictures; reading aloud to the class, to a friend, or to a family member; and so on. Writing is a very important part of the whole-language approach. Students begin by telling stories through various art media, but then they begin writing simple sentences and finally paragraphs. One of the most emphasized forms of writing is journalizing. Students write in their journals about what they are doing day-to-day. At the beginning, the teacher encourages students to express their thoughts in writing and refrains from criticizing the spelling or grammar errors. As the children become more fluent in their writing, they can work on punctuation and other skills.

Reading is especially important in the African American Sunday School because it is the means of liberation. With the ability to communicate comes empowerment. In the days when many African Americans were enslaved in the United States, teaching slaves to read was banned. Even gathering together for church became illegal. White slave masters realized that educated people who read the Bible understood that God created all people and that each one is so important to Him that He sent His only Son to die for everyone. When people discover the truth, the truth sets them free (John 8:32).

The economy of today requires educated people. Illiteracy not only threatens the economic order of a society; it also constitutes a profound injustice. This injustice has serious consequences, such as the inability of people to make good decisions for themselves or to participate in the political process (Freire and Macedo 1987, vii).

Reading can be a tool to emancipate people spiritually as well as economically. The Protestant Reformation was a good example of this. Martin Luther and other reformers made the Bible available in the language of the people and taught them how to read. No longer were the people subservient to the state church. They could now access the Father directly through His Son. Christians must be able to read God's Word for themselves to grow into spiritual maturity.

IDEAS FOR USING READING TO INCREASE SPIRITUAL GROWTH IN CHILDREN

Words can be the star in a Christian-education program, and even in the whole church program. The classroom environment can be filled with print containing information for the students, such as the class schedule, the title of the lesson, and the Bible memory verse. The teacher may even write these things on the chalkboard before class begins.

Primary classrooms often have signs everywhere labeling and identifying objects in the environment, such as "table," "door," and "piano." The students themselves can be engaged in various labeling activities, from writing their names on their Sunday School lessons to printing labels on index cards to display. The teacher may also photograph the children or let them draw pictures of themselves, and then display the pictures along with each child's name. Or the teacher may attach the photos to a poster board and label the poster "Jesus loves us."

The teacher can also communicate with students and family members in a variety of ways, such as sending individual notes to students to elicit their thoughts and opinions. Even first graders' opinions can be solicited through written questions such as, "Did you learn your memory verse?" "Was it easy?" Questions may be accompanied by pictures of various facial expressions with room for comments. This activity not only gives students an opportunity to practice their reading skills, but it also encourages them to express themselves.

Reading activities are especially applicable to Sunday School lessons for juniors, particularly with respect to the Scripture passages. As the students read a passage, they can discuss what will happen next or what might have happened if a Bible character had taken a different path. Juniors can paraphrase the memory verse in their own words; they can identify the characters, setting, goals, events, results, and resolution of a Bible story; and they can even be involved in extension activities, such as writing, art, music, and creative thinking.

The students also need opportunities to communicate with one another. The teacher writes the news on the chalkboard about what happened in their lives during the week. The class can then read the news, either silently or taking turns aloud, and they can offer edits as needed.

Reading can take place in a variety of ways. Students may silently read long passages. They may also read aloud a portion of their lesson or the Scripture passage as a group. Or the teacher may divide the children into pairs so they can read to each other. The teacher may also create opportunities for the children to read and write for special audiences. This may include reading to the church congregation during opening or closing exercises or reading to family members as part of a homework assignment. To help students understand the purpose of these activities, the teacher may say, "We need to practice reading to be good readers."

Students also need to see their teachers and others in church leadership positions learning and gathering information from a variety of written resources. Bible dictionaries, commentaries, and encyclopedias should be available, and the students should see their teachers referring to them frequently. Teachers should also use a variety of English language references. For instance, if the teacher is uncertain how to spell a word, the children should see him or her look it up in a dictionary.

WRITING TO ENHANCE SPIRITUAL GROWTH IN CHILDREN

Writing can also be incorporated into Sunday School lessons. In primary classes, the children may tell a Bible story in their own words as the teacher writes the paraphrase on the chalkboard. Even juniors will enjoy this activity if more creativity is involved, such as making up a story about a child who helped another child, with each student contributing a sentence of the story. Your students will also enjoy doing some creative writing on their own. Younger children may just write a couple of sentences with lots of "invented" spelling. Students from primary through junior age may write stories about children who are obeying the Bible, especially the teaching of that day's lesson. Then the children will enjoy reading their stories to one another. Other opportunities to write may be sending get-well notes, Valentine's Day cards, and Christmas cards. Offering students choices of written language activities further increases the enjoyment.

Different types of literature can also be used as a means of expression, such as writing poems to Mother on Mother's Day and prayers to God. The teacher may model and share with the students by writing poetry and other forms of literature, such as short stories, song lyrics, or plays. The children will also enjoy reading skits or even writing skits themselves.

Writing is particularly helpful in encouraging students to think and reflect. A teacher may give students a specified amount of time to write everything they were thinking about as they read a certain Scripture, when a particular event happened, or as they were listening to a specific Bible story. Such assignments can be used to introduce a lesson. For instance, students may be asked to think about and write three reasons why we give gifts on Christmas.

Recording information is another means of communication. Journals are an especially important means of record keeping. The children can keep track of the things they pray for and the ways God answers their prayers. They can write about times when they witness to people. Students can also use their journals as a place to express thoughts and feelings about past, current, or future events in their lives. Students may read and share entries from their journals with their teachers and with one another. Discussing written communication is very important too.

Students can also use written communication to respond to Scripture. For instance, the children may make dioramas (miniature displays) interpreting their favorite scenes from a Bible story with written explanations to accompany the displays. Additional written information may be displayed on the board with such titles as "What We Learned from This Story," "Our Favorite Part of This Lesson," and so forth. These activities will highlight for students that we communicate and respond to one another through written language.

Teachers also need to create opportunities for students to respond in writing to what they are reading in the Bible itself. For instance, teachers may model the use of written language to respond to the Bible by writing their own responses to Scripture and sharing them with their students. Beginning readers may read easy-to-read Bible story picture books and respond with drawings, or they may read and respond to very short selections from a Bible translation that is easier for them to understand. However, the important thing is to create an atmosphere in which students view written language as a beneficial means to respond to God and to life.

As we use reading and writing in our classrooms, we want our students to see that language arts are useful for spiritual growth. Teachers need to model language skills and provide opportunities for students to read and write for a variety of purposes. There are many ways to do this, such as sending home written communication through the students to the parents.

STORYTELLING TO ENHANCE SPIRITUAL GROWTH IN CHILDREN

Storytelling is a very effective way of conveying God's truth. Bible stories with interesting characters and plots are the best for storytelling. Children especially enjoy hearing familiar and well-liked Bible stories. As I mentioned earlier, before the children read from their lessons, the teacher can bring the story to life by telling it in a dramatic way. This takes some preparation, but it is well worth it. The teacher needs to study the Scripture passage and the lesson plan so thoroughly that she or he can tell the story without referring to any written material. The teacher may practice telling the story in front of a child, a spouse, or even in an empty room. The teacher can use special voices, facial expressions, and body gestures to enhance the story.

A good storyteller establishes routines that help the children get ready for a good story and put them in an expectant frame of mind. Lowering the lights and singing songs may provide an effective transition. The storyteller should be prepared and calm when he or she tells the children that a story is about to begin.

Telling Bible stories is not an either-or proposition. The teacher can also read the stories, the students can read them, or the stories can be acted out.

AN OUTLINE FOR THE CLASSROOM TEACHER

Many teachers find 6- and 7-year-olds the most difficult age level to teach because these children cannot read the lesson for themselves and teachers are afraid to use methods that may seem more suited to preschoolers. By borrowing an idea from the whole-language approach, we can see that telling or reading a story to young primaries is still part of the literacy process. Teachers can use an abundance of literacy methods to teach the lesson. In fact, if teachers will use a variety of methods to teach each lesson, this will not only reinforce the lesson for students, but it will help students take some more steps on the road toward fluent reading.

In a typical lesson, the teacher may show the children a picture of the Bible story and discuss it with them. Learning to "read" a picture is an important step in learning to read. The teacher may ask questions that will lead the children to wonder what is going to happen in the story, such as "What do you think this man is telling Jesus?" Then the teacher may tell the story in a dramatic fashion. Afterward, the teacher may point to the words on a large visual aid or point to the words on the students' papers while she or he reads. Some children may want to read the words after the teacher as they point to each word. If there are more advanced students in the class, they can be paired up with the younger children to read the lesson to each other.

Guide older children in reading silently first. The teacher can ask a few questions for the students to think about while they are reading. This style of reading helps children read for meaning rather than just reading mere words without comprehension. After the children have read the story silently, they may read it again aloud, although this is not always necessary if they demonstrate that they have understood the passage.

Children should be encouraged to learn the mechanics of Bible reading. They need to learn to recite the names of the books of the Bible in order and should be able to recognize the names of the books when they see them written out. A number of games can be played to see if the children are able to find a Bible verse. In one of the simplest games, the teacher calls out a Scripture reference, and the children race to see who can find it and read it first.

More importantly than knowing the mechanics of finding things in the Bible, children need to learn to read the Bible for themselves. One big hindrance to doing this may be that students do not read fluently enough. However, this problem can easily be resolved by assigning bite-sized portions that they can handle. For instance, younger primaries can be encouraged to read their Bible memory verse every night before they go to bed. This can become a habit that will lead to reading the Bible on a daily basis. As children develop reading fluency, they should have their own Bibles in an easy-to-read translation, such as the *Good News Bible*, the *New International Version*, or the *New Living Translation*.

Conclusion

Reading God's Word empowers us for spiritual growth, so teaching children how to read the Bible is the most important tool we can give them. Anything that will help our students become better readers can help them become better Christians. Let's apply ourselves to the task!

Reference List

Freire, Paulo and Donaldo Macedo. *Literacy: Reading the Word and the World*. South Hadley, Massachusetts: Bergin & Garvey Publishers, Inc., 1987.

CHAPTER 11

HERE'S THE PLAN

This book contains lots of helpful information for those who minister to children in the African American church. Now, in conclusion, let's look at the elements of a good lesson. (A sample lesson plan is also included at the end of this chapter.) We can outline the lesson as follows:

I.   Introducing the Bible Lesson
II. Teaching the Lesson
III. Applying the Lesson
IV. Reviewing the Lesson

INTRODUCING THE BIBLE LESSON

When Leticia arrives at Sunday School today, she may be thinking about her new dress and the special hairdo her mother created for her. Rolando may be thinking about the fight he had with his brother on the way to church. And Chonda is worrying about the big fight her mother and father had the night before.

You may want to start class with devotions or prayer or even, "Class, turn to page 10 in your student quarterlies." However, if you do not have the attention of your students, your words may not be accomplishing what you think they are. The minds of your students may be so far away from the class that they do not hear a word you are saying.

Two objectives need to be accomplished at the beginning of any lesson. First, you must get the attention of the students. And second, you must help students see that the lesson will be relevant to their lives. Good teachers always seek to get the attention of their students before beginning their lessons. Maybe a little prayer is said, but then we must be sure our students are listening. (You may want to save the prayer until just before plunging into the lesson in order to pray in accord with the lesson objectives.) Without accomplishing the first objective, it will be impossible to accomplish the second.

An Attention-Getting Activity

An attention-getting activity for primaries may be an active game, such as Follow the Leader. This game introduces the idea of following so that the children will understand what you mean when you tell them to follow Jesus. This activity is not only a fun way to introduce the lesson, but it is also a way to incorporate an important biblical concept that reinforces the Scripture passage for that week's lesson. After the children play the game, it's time to discuss and reflect on following Jesus.

Juniors also enjoy captivating ways to introduce the lesson. A discussion of who they would most like to emulate would introduce this same lesson on following for juniors. You might ask such questions as "Why would you want to be like this person?" or "What things would you do to be like them?" Juniors like to talk and express their opinions and ideas, and this discussion would help them reflect on what qualities and behaviors are good ones to emulate.

A Life-Relevancy Story

Once you have your students' attention, you will then tell them a story about a child their age who wants to follow a hero—perhaps a parent, a celebrity athlete, or another hero or heroine. As you talk about ways the child in the story will follow the "leader," your students will better understand what it means to follow Jesus Christ. As the children learn about the different ways they can follow Jesus, they will become interested in what the Bible lesson has to say about following our Lord.

Sometimes, especially with juniors and older students, you may begin the lesson with a single activity that will not only get their attention but will also show them how the Scripture passage is relevant to their lives. A well-told story will do this, but if your students are simply reading the story from their lesson books, you may need to consider some ways to boost the excitement so that your students do not become bored with the routine. For instance, you may introduce the reading with some questions, such as "Did you ever forget to do something your mother told you to do? What happened?" or "Let's read about a girl who was supposed to be home by five o'clock but was very late."

Another alternative would be to pantomime something from the story and ask the children to guess what you are doing. Then guide them in reading the story about contemporary juniors who are facing the same kinds of issues that they face.

A third idea is to begin the class with a discussion of the things that are happening in the lives of your students. Such discussions are especially important when significant things have happened, such as a holiday, the beginning of a new school year, or even some tragedy in the news like the murder of a child. We need to help our students process what is happening in their lives so they can see that God cares about them, that He has something to say to them, and that coming to class will help them understand those things that concern them. When we can guide our students from these discussions of their own lives into the Bible lesson for the day, we have given the most significant introduction to our lesson that is possible.

In order to use the happenings in the learners' lives as a springboard for the lesson, you will need to do some in-depth thinking and praying beforehand. Think about the challenges your students are facing today and then think about the lesson in Scripture. What truths in that passage speak to these challenges?

TEACHING THE LESSON

Now we are ready to teach the Sunday School lesson, which is based upon a Scripture passage. In chapter 7 we talked about using objectives. Teaching objectives are derived from observing a particular need in the lives of our students and connecting this need to what the Scripture in the lesson is teaching. Let's see how we teach that Scripture to our students. Although we will make extensive use of written curriculum to teach the lesson, we can also incorporate telling a Bible story into our methods.

Telling the Bible Story

The heart of a lesson is the Bible story. As we discussed earlier, African Americans come from a cultural tradition of oral storytelling, and the history of Black people was passed down through stories. Consequently, the storyteller has always had a special position in the African American community. In the days of slavery, the Black church was often denied the right to read the Bible, but in spite of this, the stories of the Word were still taught through the Black preacher. Even today most African American preachers retain this special gift of bringing to life the stories of the Bible.

Written Sunday School or Vacation Bible School curriculum was never meant to replace the telling of Bible stories. Primaries, in particular, do not read their lessons with great fluency or dramatic inflection, so they not only need to review the lesson by reading their student folders, but they first need to hear the story from their teacher. After they have both heard and read the story, primaries can then tell the story themselves—verbally, dramatically, or in art form.

Do not assume that just because juniors can read the Scripture passage for themselves there is not great value in telling the story to them before or after they have read it. A well-told story will make the Bible come alive for your students, and it will keep alive a wonderful African tradition.

Also, since the reading skills of juniors are advancing, they can learn to be the storytellers. Once they have read the Scripture passage silently, they will then be able to tell the story to their classmates. Learning to tell the stories themselves gives juniors the important responsibility of interpreting Scripture for themselves. This is also an excellent way for teachers to discover how students understand the lesson so that they can provide further guidance in areas where students have not grasped the essentials.

How can you as a teacher prepare to tell a Bible story? After asking the Lord to help you to understand the Scripture passage, read it several times in a variety of translations. Be sure to make use of Bible commentaries and dictionaries to help you grasp the meaning. When you read the passage, seek to understand it first in a general way, thinking about what the passage is really all about. Then think about how you can apply the Scripture to your own life.

Now you are ready to prepare for teaching the children. Notice the details in the story. Think about which of these details would be more interesting and relevant to the children in your class. Think about the sounds, the smells, the feelings, and the sights that you imagine may have been part of the story. Notice the characters in the story. Think about their personalities. How did they respond? How might they have felt? What did they say? What did they do? While being very careful not to add to Scripture or take away from it, what are some details that are surely part of the story that are not directly mentioned?

Focus on those parts of the story to which your students will be most able to relate. Bring out the parts of children or young people. Emphasize family relationships and other situations that your children will understand. Think of the elements that make up a good story. A story needs a hook, a plot, personality development, and a theme. It catches the listener's attention right from the beginning, and the excitement continues throughout the story, all the while building up to the climax. A good story also has an interesting plot—something happens throughout the course of the story that the listener wants to know more about. The plot is developed through the characters of the story. Some of the characters have personalities that children can relate to, some may be obvious villains, and some may undergo changes in the course of the story. However, the most important element of a story is the theme or objective for its use in the classroom. The objective may be very obvious, or it may be almost hidden and needs to be drawn out.

Go to the library and read some of the children's favorite storybooks to see what makes a successful story. The difference between a poorly told story and an exciting story is often in the details. Carefully study the Scripture passage you will be teaching. There are often interesting details you may not notice at first. Notice in Jesus' ordination service (Luke 4:16–26) that Jesus stood up to read the Scripture and then sat down to teach about its message. (This is true in West African teaching today.) Notice the detailed description of the things Jesus said He would do. You may dramatically act out each of the details. Mention how surprised the people were to hear this great message from Jesus, who had grown up in their community.

Another element of good stories, especially for children, is repetition. Never use "and so on" in a good story! The children enjoy anticipating what comes next, especially if you invite them to say some of these things with you. Look at the story of Jesus telling three men to follow Him (Luke 9:57–62). You may say the words "Follow me" as Jesus calls each of the men. Maybe you will want to turn to the children then and say, "Follow me." And if there is time, repeat the stories each week. Children love to hear a good story over and over.

Imagine what things sounded like, smelled like, looked like, and felt like. Think of the Christmas story about Mary and Joseph as they looked for a place to stay so that Mary could have her baby (Luke 2:1–6). They had traveled a hot, dusty road. They were tired and dirty. They looked for a place to stay but could find no room in the inn. As you tell the story, you may talk about the donkey clip-clopping along. Talk about the smell of the animals in the stable. Look around to see the camels, the cows, and the sheep. Listen to the sounds: the moos, the baahs, and even the cries of little Baby Jesus.

Use dramatic gestures in telling a Bible story. Think of John the Baptist preaching to the crowd (Matthew 3:1–6). Use your own pastor's gestures as you tell the boys and girls what John had to say to the people. Think of how Mary may have felt when the angel made his announcement to her that she would soon give birth to the Son of God (Luke 1:26–37). Show Mary's surprise with your arms, your hands, and your eyes. Act out the shepherds' response as they excitedly ran to Bethlehem to see the wonderful Baby the angels sang about (Luke 2:8–20).

After you have figured out how to tell the story, rehearse it. Some people rehearse it aloud when they are home alone, but most find it best to rehearse it by telling it to their own children, family members, or friends. Rehearse it until you can tell it smoothly.

The most important preparation for telling a good Bible story is to read it, meditate upon it, and rehearse it with prayer! God bless you as you tell the wonderful stories of our glorious Lord!

Teaching the Bible Memory Verse

Primaries and juniors are at an age when their memorizing abilities are increasing. Memorization is a mental exercise, and so children profit from increasing this brain activity. Most importantly, memorization is also a commandment of Scripture. Moses told the people, "These commandments that I give you today are to be upon your hearts" (Deuteronomy 6:6). Research shows that children memorize better when they learn a Scripture verse as a whole rather than breaking it down into parts. However, not everyone learns in the same way, and variety is always helpful, so we suggest that you use a variety of ways to teach the verses to your students.

The first principle is to make sure your students understand the Scripture passage. Explain any words that might be unfamiliar. You may even want to explain whole phrases. Then ask for a volunteer to put the whole verse in his or her own words. This way you will find out whether the children really understand the verse.

The second principle is to help your students memorize the verse. Although there are many memorization techniques, the most common method is to read the verse together about five times and then recite it from memory. Another way is to divide the verse into phrases and learn one phrase at a time. (Always make sure students memorize the reference as well. If the children say the reference before and after the verse, they will be better able to remember it.)

Sometimes it is fun to use a game to help students memorize the verse. The most common game is to write the verse on the board, read it through once, and then ask a child to erase one word. Then the children read the verse, supplying from memory the missing word. Repeat the procedure until all the words are erased and the children can say the verse from memory.

There are many other games for memorizing Bible verses. Just read your lesson plans for a variety of ideas.

APPLYING THE LESSON

Applying the lesson is just as important as learning the content, and there are a variety of ways to help your students apply God's truth to their lives. The first step is figuring out how to apply it. We cannot just assume that students will put the Word into practice, especially if they are unsure how to do so. When we talk about telling others about Christ, children need help to know what to say. When we talk about being kind, primaries, especially, will need to think through some ways of demonstrating kindness. Always be sure that the children can tell you some ways to apply the lesson of the day.

It is often helpful to use paper-and-pencil activities or workbook activities to clarify the application. These are included in well-prepared curriculum by Christian publishers. When you introduce these activities, talk about the best answers before the students write in their answers. This does not mean that you will give them the answers. Ask the children first, but correct them if needed, before they write in the wrong answers. This will reinforce the right answers. Then be sure to give them class time to actually write in the answers. The act of writing in the answers not only reinforces learning, but it ensures that all the students under-stand the answers.

The second step of application is putting the lesson into practice right away. A good lesson gives students an opportunity to decide how they will immediately put into practice the things they have learned. John Dewey, a renowned American educator, said that "learning is doing." Those things we do immediately are the first step toward making biblical application a habit. Sometimes we encourage students to "say something kind to someone each day this week" or to repeat some other action each day. This is an even better way to make biblical application a habit, because students are repeating a Christianlike habit over and over.

During class time, it is sometimes hard for students to actually do what the Scrip-ture tells us to do. So in these circumstances, we can only remind them about the specific action and ask them to commit to practicing it later. For more reinforce-ment, students can role-play many of these actions during class. When children act out the right actions, they are making good behaviors part of their own reper-toire of things they can do to please God. Children can act out what to do when they see other children bullying someone; they can act out inviting someone to Vacation Bible School; or they can rehearse what they will pray when they do something wrong.

However, some biblical truths can be put into practice right away. For instance, when a student is sick, the children can make get-well cards. To help feed the hungry, they can bring cans of food for the church food pantry. Children can also begin treating one another with love and respect. A class on giving should inspire them to give all they have in their pockets.

The practical suggestions in this section will not only help students apply the teaching of God's Word, but they are also helpful tools for getting the attention of your students, for introducing a new series of lessons, or for reviewing the material students have already learned. Now let's look at crafts and bulletin boards.

The Place of Crafts in the Classroom

Crafts are fun and most children love them; however, the purpose of crafts is not just for fun. Learning takes place in many ways. We learn with our ears and eyes, but we also learn with our hands.

Studies have shown that each of us has a different learning style. Think of some different ways we memorize a Bible verse. Some of us learn best by singing the verse that is set to a tune. Some memorize the verse by reading it to themselves. Others learn by listening to others say the verse. Still others will learn quickest if the words are written on blocks that they must manipulate into the correct position. How do you best remember a new name? Do you need to see that name written down? Do you use a clever trick to remember, such as a funny word that rhymes with that name? Do you write the name on a slip of paper and stick it to your mirror or refrigerator?

Children have different ways of learning too. Some have high spatial-relationship intelligence. This means that they remember things they see laid out in the spaces of a piece of artwork. They learn by moving things around in spaces, such as by drawing pictures of themselves sharing or opening the windows in a craft to see the answers underneath. For these children, it is especially important to make crafts a part of the total curriculum. They will grow up to be car mechanics, brain surgeons, artists, and architects if we help them value their skills and give them opportunities to develop their special intelligence. An important part of our mission as teachers is to help children discover the gifts God has given them. The child who can paint something or build something has a gift from God that he or she needs to learn to utilize for God's glory.

We tend to think of teaching as just using words—spoken, heard, written, and read. Yet some things must be learned in other ways. For instance, we can only learn of the love of God by experiencing His love. Students experience God's love through caring teachers who know them by name and speak words of encouragement to them. They feel God's love through a teacher's smile and a hug or two. God's love is also expressed in songs and in the things teachers do to make the classroom an attractive and welcoming place.

Learning what the Bible says is important, but we also want children to obey the Word. We can tell the children to do the things God tells us to do, but it is far better to give them the opportunity to put the teaching into practice right in the classroom. Give the children opportunities to make things for others. This experience in giving is a far better teacher than just telling our students to show love to others through giving and sharing. Children can also make invitations for Vacation Bible School or Sunday School. In doing this, our students will be learning to witness to others. Always remember that the teaching method must be suited to the learning objective.

Another reason why crafts are a necessary part of Christian education is that students retain best the things they do and discover for themselves. For instance, children can discover through a game they themselves have made that playing fairly is more fun. They can also discover that giving something to someone else brings joy to the giver as well as the recipient.

A final reason for doing crafts is because primary and junior children are at an age when the skills they use while constructing crafts will form the foundation for other skills they will develop later on. Children need to master fine (finger) muscle dexterity required for academic skills, such as printing, cursive writing, and even creating models for understanding beginning geometry.

Young children in Africa are learning to weave baskets, carve wood, and make other useful and beautiful crafts. These skills help the brain develop. Learning takes place in steps. Most 4-year-olds can hold scissors and be taught to cut straight lines, and most 5-year-olds can learn to follow a simple line and direct the path as they cut along.

Many children who were deprived of opportunities to use scissors as preschoolers and kindergartners have difficulties with the cutting projects in first grade. They also have trouble with the finger control necessary for printing and cursive writing in the first through fourth grades. These kinds of difficulties are preventable if teachers of young children incorporate crafts into their lessons. Moreover, for primaries and juniors who already have these kinds of difficulties, crafts can enable children to overcome them and make progress in their development. Yes, crafts are fun, and even fun is an important part of the Sunday School curriculum. And, yes, crafts are messy and can be a lot of work for the teacher, but we want children to enjoy coming to class and to learn by whatever means are best. So let's give our children the many benefits of doing crafts in Sunday School.

Bulletin-Board Bonanza

Many of us lead hectic lives nowadays. Sunday School teachers find that Sunday mornings are always rushed. Vacation Bible Schools are less and less the leisurely morning adventures they once were and more and more are becoming evening schools because most of the teachers are working during the days. The idea of making a special effort to come to class early on Sundays or devoting a special period of time to work on bulletin boards is often pushed to the back of our minds. But if you are willing to put the extra effort into well-planned bulletin boards—even if it means getting up half an hour earlier on Sunday morning or coming to church sometime during the week—you will find the quality of your teaching greatly enhanced.

A bulletin board is meant to emphasize a theme in a visual way, because we are much more likely to remember the things we see than the things we just hear. The first characteristic of a good bulletin board is that it accomplishes specific teaching objectives. It may help students remember the factual material of the Bible lessons or understand how to apply the Bible teaching to their lives or initiate interest in the lessons. Think about the purpose of the bulletin board as you are creating it. Identifying the purpose will help you know how best to use it.

A second characteristic of a good bulletin board is that it is interactive. One of the best ways to get around your time-crunch problems is to invite the children to help you make the bulletin board. As you and your students are tacking up the pieces, weave in questions and discussion that will help accomplish the teachings of that particular display. In addition to helping you tack pieces on the bulletin board, the children can be involved in making some of the components. A bulletin board on the family may include drawings of your students' families; a Christmas bulletin board may include pictures of gifts that the children may give Jesus; and so forth. The wonderful thing about including the children in making drawings for the bulletin board is that this makes the material more applicable to your students than any commercially prepared materials ever could be.

Another way to create interactive bulletin boards is similar to what we are seeing at many museums nowadays. Most museum exhibits are no longer static displays. Think about the ways large museums attract visitors through interactive learning. We can do the same sort of things with our bulletin boards. Maybe there are flaps that must be opened to see the answers to questions, or strings to attach to match the correct items, or items to move to indicate the progression toward goals.

Following a couple of simple guidelines will help you create successful Sunday School bulletin boards. (Some churches do not have bulletin boards, but teachers can create them by making borders on the walls with masking tape.) First, make sure that the board hangs at the eye level of your students. Second, make the creation of the bulletin board an ongoing process for you and your students. For instance, each week you may want to add a picture of something new that relates specifically to that week's lesson. One year I created a special seasonal bulletin board titled "God Gives Us Seasons." I cut out a tree trunk from a large grocery bag and tacked it to the center of the bulletin board. In the springtime, the children helped cut out green leaves from construction paper, and we tacked all the leaves on the tree, adding a few more each week until the tree was full for summertime. In the fall, we replaced the green leaves with colorful autumn leaves. In October, we gradually took the leaves off the tree and tacked them to the ground around the base of the tree. When winter came, we put cotton-ball "snow" in the air, on the ground, and on the branches of the tree. Bulletin boards are such a special teaching aid that I enjoy having two of them in my classroom!

However, we do not need to limit classroom visual aids to the bulletin board. By using the masking-tape method of attaching visuals to the walls, we can create a truly beautiful classroom. The children may cut colorful autumn leaves out of construction paper and tape them all over the walls. Another successful idea for many teachers is to get a large roll of mural paper, butcher paper, or blank newsprint and cut out lengths of paper at least the height of each student. Next, ask each student to lie down on his or her piece of paper so you can trace all around the child to create a whole-body silhouette. Then have the children color their silhouettes and cut them out. Use masking tape to hang them on the walls, and include a sign that says, "Jesus loves me." This is a lengthy activity that is best done on a Saturday when there is more time or as part of the day camp or morning Vacation Bible School curriculum.

Some additional tips will help you make an attractive and educationally stimulating atmosphere in your classroom. First, do not keep visuals up too long, unless you are continually changing the display to keep it interesting and relevant. Bulletin boards can become unattractive and outdated, making the children lose interest in looking at them. Second, keep your classroom neat. An orderly classroom helps children become more organized in their own approaches to learning. A neat classroom also reflects your respect for the house of the Lord.

REVIEWING THE LESSON

African American Sunday School teachers have always done a wonderful job reviewing the lesson because they know the importance of what they are teaching. When you teach a lesson, you need to ask questions that continually challenge students to remember what you have taught. Likewise, when you begin a new lesson, it should always include a review of the previous lesson. Your review approach should involve more than just answering questions, because, as we know, that type of review primarily tests cognitive learning—the learning of biblical facts. When we go beyond questions in our review of the lesson, we will help our students remember how to live what the Bible teaches and love the Lord.

Challenging our students to apply God's Word to their lives involves reviewing their commitments with them. The week after we study the importance of reading God's Word on a daily basis, we may review with juniors what they have done in their personal Bible reading. When we study the importance of helping, we may ask primaries to take home a checklist, have their parents give them checks when they help around the house that week, and then return the paper the following week so we can talk about how they did. Because children tend to be very forgetful, we may need to call them during the week to remind them of their commitments or provide a little treat for those who return to class with their finished lessons.

A review of the lessons of the heart is an especially treasured experience. Maybe your students finished class with a heartfelt singing of "I Have Decided to Follow Jesus." The following week you may sing this song again to remind the children of their promises to follow the Lord.

Well, now we are ready. Let's teach!

APPENDIX

SAMPLE LESSON PLAN

Title: The Way You Act

Based on: Acts 3:1–16

Lesson Objectives

Knowledge: That primaries will know that Peter healed a crippled man through the power of Jesus.

Attitude: That primaries will feel compassionate toward those needing their help.

Action: That primaries will do something kind for someone this week.

I. INTRODUCING THE LESSON

A. Get attention activity

Ask your students questions about physically challenged people they have seen begging. Explain that we call people who cannot see or hear or walk physically challenged. You might ask students the following questions: Have you ever seen a blind person or a crippled person begging for money? Were they selling something? Were they playing music? What were they doing? Why do you think they were begging? Could a blind person work for money? Could a crippled person have a job? Cite examples of things that physically challenged people can do, but mention that it is harder for physically challenged people to get jobs. Then tell the children, "In Bible days a physically challenged person could not work. The only way the person could get money for food and clothes was by begging."

B. Primary children's story

When Stephanie had to start a new school, she felt very lonely. But one of the girls came over to be her friend.

"Hi, my name's Angela. Welcome to Douglass School."

Angela showed Stephanie around the school and invited her to join the other girls during recess.

Stephanie asked Angela, "Hey, are you a Christian?"

"Yes," said Angela. "How did you know?"

"Oh, by the way you act so kind and friendly," said Stephanie.

How can you tell if a person is a Christian? Why is it important for Christians to be kind to other people?

II. TEACHING THE LESSON

A. Telling the Bible story

(Use a Bible story picture as a visual aid.)

After Jesus went back to heaven, Peter and John, His apostles, continued going to the temple to worship God. Often, blind or crippled people would beg by the gate of the temple. One day Peter and John saw a man there who had been crippled since he was born. When the man begged Peter and John for money, they looked right at him and said, "Look at us!"

The man looked at them thinking they were going to give him something. Then Peter told him that he had no money, but that he was going to give him something better. Peter said, "In the name of Jesus Christ of Nazareth, walk."

Peter took the man's hand and lifted him up. Right away, the man's legs and feet got strong. He jumped up in the air and began thanking God. He went into the temple with Peter and John, still thanking God.

The people who saw him walking and praising God were amazed. They knew that he had never been able to walk before. They all began running to the porch of the temple so they could hear about what had happened. "Why does this surprise you?" asked Peter. "The same God who raised Jesus from the dead made this man walk" (Acts 3:12, 16, NIV author's paraphrase). This was a wonderful miracle. Many more people believed in Jesus. They could see His power, and they could see that the Christians were kind and compassionate.

B. Memory verse (p. 3)

"Be kind and compassionate to one another" (from Ephesians 4:32).

Explain the verse to the children: "The people listened to Peter and John because they had seen Peter heal the crippled man. People will know you are a Christian if you act like one." Tell the children that when you are compassionate, you think about how difficult things are for others and feel sorry when they are sad. Ask the children to say the word *compassionate* three times.

Work on memorizing the verse together: Ask the boys to read the verse together, and then have the girls respond by saying the verse again. Then ask all the children to read the reference together. Do this several times until the children can recite the verse and reference from memory.

III. APPLYING THE LESSON

A. Discussion

Encourage each child to think of something he or she could do this week to show kindness to someone. Ask the children to tell the class their plans. Pray together, asking God to help them do those things.

B. Crafts

Make scrapbook pages for a shut-in. Take photos of your students, let them draw pictures, or give them magazines with colorful pictures to cut out. Give each child a page and provide the children with stamps, stickers, and whatever scrapbook-making materials you have available. Combine all the pages together to form the scrapbook. Be sure to take the scrapbook to a shut-in this week.

IV. REVIEWING THE LESSON

A. Visual aids

Display the Bible story picture and ask questions, such as, "What was wrong with this man?" "How did Peter help him?" Recite the memory verse together and then ask for volunteers to recite the memory verse individually.

B. Worship time

After singing some favorite songs—such as "Jesus Loves Me"—that tell us of Jesus' love, teach the song "They Will Know We Are Christians by Our Love."

Close with a prayer: "Dear Lord, help us show others that we love You by the ways we show love to them. Amen."